SURVIVING
YOUR PARENTS'
DIVORCE

ALSO AVAILABLE IN THE WILEY LEGAL AND
PRACTICAL GUIDE SERIES:

Surviving Your Divorce: A Guide to Canadian Family Law, Second Edition, by
Michael G. Cochrane (ISBN: 0-471-64399-8)

*For Better or For Worse: The Canadian Guide to Marriage
Contracts and Cohabitation Agreements* by Michael G. Cochrane
(ISBN: 0-471-64206-1)

*Facing A Death in the Family: Caring for Someone Through Illness and Dying,
Arranging the Funeral, Dealing with the Will and Estate* by Margaret Kerr and
JoAnn Kurtz (ISBN: 0-471-64396-3)

The Complete Guide to Buying, Owning and Selling a Home in Canada by
Margaret Kerr and JoAnn Kurtz (ISBN: 0-471-64191-X)

*You Be The Judge: The Complete Canadian Guide to Resolving Legal Disputes Out of
Court* by Norman A. Ross (ISBN: 0-471-64199-5)

SURVIVING YOUR PARENTS' DIVORCE

A Guide for Young Canadians

SECOND EDITION

Michael G. Cochrane, LL.B.

JOHN WILEY & SONS CANADA, LTD

Toronto · New York · Chichester · Weinheim · Brisbane · Singapore

John Wiley & Sons Canada, Ltd
22 Worcester Road
Etobicoke, Ontario
M9W 1L1

Canadian Cataloguing in Publication Data

Cochrane, Michael G. (Michael George), 1953-
    Surviving your parents' divorce : a guide for young Canadians

(A Wiley legal and practical guide)
2nd ed.
Includes index.
ISBN 0-471-64398-X

1. Divorce — Juvenile literature. 2. Divorce — Law and legislation — Canada — Juvenile literature. I. Title II. Series.

HQ814.C63 1999   j306.89   C99-930439-9

Production Credits
Cover Design: Interrobang Graphic Design Inc.
Text Design: Natalia Burobina
Printer: Tri-Graphic Printing Ltd.

Printed in Canada
10 9 8 7 6 5 4 3 2 1

CONTENTS

ACKNOWLEDGMENTS

I would like to thank and acknowledge the contribution of the many children I have met during my legal career in family law. Their questions and observations on separation and divorce and how it affects their parents have provided some profound insight into the divorce experience in Canada.

Thanks also to my daughter, who, as a budding author herself, is an honest critic and a constant inspiration. Thanks Emma.

Michael G. Cochrane, B.A. LL. B.

AUTHOR'S NOTE TO PARENTS

This book is designed to help young people learn about a number of aspects of divorce and separation in Canada. Hundreds of thousands of Canadian parents divorce every year and tens of thousands of children are affected.

The adults do what they must with their lawyers and counsellors. While the adults may be heartbroken or angry, they usually understand the process of divorce as they move through it.

Children, on the other hand, do not understand what is happening. They are often left in the dark, sometimes used as pawns by those same brokenhearted and angry adults. I believe that, with the information in this book, young people will be able to understand what is happening to the adults in their lives and cope with the stress and conflict that are often part of divorce. If we expect Canadian children to emerge from divorce as healthy and happy people then we have to help them understand the process, both legally and emotionally. This is my small contribution based on what I've learned from my years as a family-law lawyer, mediator and from my own experience as a parent who has been through a divorce himself.

The information here is presented in plain language and addressed directly to young people. It is the unvarnished truth. Nobody can pick out a "B.S. artist" faster than a kid, so I tell them everything I think they need to know as honestly as I can. There is nothing in this book that will harm or disturb a child whose parents are going through a divorce. Far more harm will come from not giving children accurate information. Some children will end up knowing more about divorce than most adults after reading this book. That's not a bad thing. I have met quite a few parents who have something to learn from their children.

Having said all of that, this book does not contain legal advice. It does, however, contain legal information. Advice is when a lawyer tells a client how the law may apply to the client's situation. The only advice I give kids is to stop blaming themselves for what their parents are doing.

As an adult, if you are worried about the contents of the book then read it yourself. I am confident of three things if you do. First, you will want your child to read it. Second, you will learn more about what your child is thinking about during the divorce process. Third, you may learn more about Canadian divorce yourself. If you feel you need still more information for yourself, read my book *Surviving Your Divorce: A Guide to Canadian Family Law*, also published by John Wiley & Sons.

1 INTRODUCTION

If you picked up this book there must be a reason. You know the book is about "divorce" from the title, so...

Maybe you're doing a school assignment.

Maybe a friend of yours mentioned that his or her parents were talking about splitting up or separating or finally getting divorced.

Or maybe your cousin, your aunt or uncle or someone else in your family has talked about divorce and you are a little curious.

Or...maybe it is happening in your family. Are your mother and father talking about divorce? Do you hear them discussing it when they think you can't hear? Most parents seem to think that no one knows they are even considering it. Or they may be screaming at each other and don't care if the whole world knows. This can be pretty tense for you. It can even be a little embarrassing. But the worst part is not knowing what is going to happen next. Am I right?

You may have brothers and sisters, in fact, you probably do since most families in Canada have more than one child. If your brothers or sisters are not too young, say less than five years old, then you may want to talk to them about what is going on. Your older brothers and sisters may have more information but probably don't know everything that's in this book. In either case, they may be worried...just like you...and need someone to talk to. The point of this book is to help fill in some of the blanks.

There is information here that probably your mom and dad don't even know. If you know what the divorce laws are all about then you can ask the right questions or, if someone asks you a question, you might just blow them away with what you learn here. There is nothing like a little knowledge... oops, I'm starting to sound like one of your teachers.

Also, if you read and understand the stuff in this book then you can pass the information on to your brothers or sisters, or your friends, or your cousin or your mom and dad. The more that everyone knows about the process of divorce, the better.

I should also mention that this book is not just for families who are thinking about divorce. It is also for families who have already separated. Sometimes your mom or your dad moves out very suddenly. This book will still help you see what is going on.

As you already know, not all parents are married to each other. Sometimes a man and a woman will live together, have children and do everything that married people do but never actually get married. This book still applies to that type of family, where the parents are in a common-law relationship. So don't stop reading just because your mom and dad or her or his partner are not married.

And another thing, it doesn't matter where you live in Canada, this book still applies. Halifax, Nova Scotia? That's OK. Vancouver, British Columbia? Fine. Regina, Saskatchewan? No problem. Ontario, Quebec, Alberta, Manitoba, New Brunswick, Newfoundland and Prince Edward Island. It even applies in the Yukon and the Northwest Territories, because the laws for separation and divorce are the same across Canada. So is the emotional process that you and your parents are going through.

WHY SHOULD I BELIEVE YOU?

Let me take a couple of pages to answer a question that some of you may have... "Why should I believe you?"

Answer: I've been there. I'm a lawyer who, in one way or another, has been working with people and divorces for over 20 years. First, I went to school for what seemed like about 200 years (actually about 8 years just studying law). Then I worked as a lawyer helping husbands and wives with their divorces. After I did that I went to work for the Ontario Ministry of the Attorney General, the government department that creates new laws and changes existing ones. I worked there for about 8 years and helped with the design of some important new family laws. While I worked for the Attorney General in Ontario, I also worked on some projects that involved people from all over Canada. (Family laws are almost the same from province to province.) I worked with those people to try and make sure that each province approached family law in pretty much the same way. As a result, I have been in every province and territory in Canada and have talked to thousands of people about divorce. For a few years I even had a chance to teach at a couple of universities.

After all the laws about separation and divorce were changed around 1986, I wrote a couple of books about family law. One of the books is for lawyers and their assistants and is probably too technical to interest you. The other book is for adults who are going through a divorce or have other problems related to divorce. That second book is called *Surviving Your Divorce: A Guide to Canadian Family Law*, and it is really for parents. While I was writing that book, I got the idea for another book about divorce that young people could read — not little kids, but someone about your age. I thought, if I could explain all this stuff to kids whose parents are going through divorces and separations, then kids might understand what their parents are going through. They might also be able to help their parents out a bit.

In the middle of all of this I switched jobs. I went back to being a lawyer in private practice who helped people with their divorces. I also started to work as a lawyer for children. No kidding. In some cases children involved in a divorce actually get to have their own lawyer. This made me think even more about how someone like you might need a book like this.

Aside from all this, I am also a parent (my daughter is a teenager now) and I am divorced from my daughter's mom. So I have been through all this stuff myself. Her mom got married again and has two more children. We are all good friends and live on the same street. That is the way it should be, but it is not always the way that it ends up for other families.

So when you ask "Why should I believe you?" think about all the things I have just mentioned and trust me, I have been there. I don't pretend to know everything about the law, but I know enough to help you. And just in case you wonder what I look like, that's my picture on the back cover.

OK so far? Now, take a look at the table of contents and see if there is anything that really interests you. Maybe you should read that topic right away. Go ahead. If you are not in a big rush, then read through the book a chapter or a section at a time. There are a few places where you might want to answer some questions. No, it's not a test. The questions are to make you think a little about your situation and to look at some of the choices you may have. All of this is important in making sure you don't get shortchanged while your parents are worrying about their problems.

Ready to start? Let's go!

2 CANADIAN KIDS AND DIVORCE: It's Not Your Fault

SHOCKING TRUTH REVEALED! MANY FAMILIES EXPERIENCE DIVORCE! Is it really that shocking? Is it a big secret that many Canadians must live through divorce? I hope you don't think so because tens of thousands of Canadians have been through it, lots of books and magazine articles have been written about it, and sometimes it seems that everyone is talking about separation and divorce.

Many children whose parents are thinking about separating or who are right in the middle of a divorce somehow get the feeling that they are alone. They feel kind of embarrassed, almost ashamed that their parents are getting divorced. The worst possible thing will happen — they will be different from their friends. Nothing can be worse than being different.

The good news is that just because your parents decide to separate and get a divorce does not mean that you're different from other young people. Every year in Canada there are about 80,000 divorces. That means about 160,000 husbands and wives become ex-husbands and ex-wives. Some of those divorces are for people who do not have kids. In fact, people with kids are less likely to divorce than people without kids. But there are many marriages where there are children that do experience divorce. How many? Would you believe that every year in Canada more than 75,000 children are caught up in divorces? That is every year.

Between the time you entered Grade 4 and the time you graduate (we hope) from high school about 675,000 Canadian kids are going to be thinking about the same things that you are thinking about. This means not only that you are not different, but also that you are not alone. Look around your classroom, your sports teams, your clubs and just among your friends and family. Lots of these kids come from families that have gone through divorce, are now going through divorce or will be going through it in the near future.

I coached a girls' baseball team called the Rockies. Most of the girls in the league are between the ages of 9 and 13, and there are about 90 girls in the whole league. We practise and play games at least once a week, and sometimes twice, so I get to see a lot of the kids who play. I started to notice the number of girls in the league who come from families that are separated, divorced, and, in some cases, remarried into stepfamilies. I have never heard anybody talk or act like this was the least bit unusual. I think all the coaches realize that it is just the way the community is today.

The same is true for teachers. They got used to the idea of divorce a long time ago. They know that many families need two copies of the school reports, permission forms, notices about open houses, and all that other stuff that gets jammed in the bottom of your knapsack. For teachers, this is no big deal.

It's the same for family doctors, dentists, bank managers, farmers, business people, grocery store owners, lawyers, and anyone else. And you know why it is not a big deal? Their families are going through the same thing. It doesn't matter whether you are rich or poor or in between, whether you are black, white, Asian, South American, Aboriginal, African, Chinese or whatever. It doesn't matter where you live in Canada. Big, small, skinny, tall, heavy, bald, beautiful, athletic or not, anyone can get divorced. Hey, it happened to me. And now it is happening to you. Join the club.

Startling Evidence Uncovered! It's Not The Kids' Fault! Get ready for another shocker!

One of the most amazing things about divorce is the number of young people who think that somehow, in the middle of all the other stuff that's been going on in the family, they are the ones who actually caused their parents to split up. Of all the thousands of kids whose parents divorce (and remember that is almost 75,000 kids each year in Canada) most of them think that they are responsible. Let's get one thing straight right now: **It's not your fault.**

Of all the thousands of situations I have seen over the last 20 years where families were having problems, not once was the divorce caused by the children. Not once.

OK, we know now that it's not your fault but that only raises two more questions:

1. If it is not your fault, then whose fault is it?
2. Why do kids *think* that it is their fault?

Both are very interesting questions, but let's deal with the second one first.

WHY DO CHILDREN BLAME THEMSELVES FOR DIVORCE?

Let's think about your classroom at school for a minute. No classroom is perfect and no teacher is perfect, and sometimes a class of kids can get a little out of control. Now I'm sure that this has never happened in *your* class and I'm sure *you* have never actually caused it to happen. You probably just keep studying when this kind of stuff happens. Yeah, right. But, imagine for a second your classroom and a teacher that made you — just you — leave the room every time he or she wanted to talk about how the class was getting out of control. After a while, you'd start to think that they were talking about you when you were out of the room. You'd probably think that they were blaming you for all the trouble. You might even start acting differently when they finally let you come back in. You might start trying to be "extra good" or you might feel hurt that you were being blamed unfairly. Or you might start acting up thinking, "Hey, I'm getting blamed anyway." Imagine if every time you tried to talk about it the teacher pretended that nothing was wrong.

It can be the same with parents who are separating. They have a problem and it's obvious. They are either yelling at each other or doing the "silent treatment" where no one speaks. I don't know which is worse. Both are awful. Sometimes when they can't get along in front of the children they start to avoid each other. Your dad may come home late or stay away for the weekend. Your mom may try to be out when your dad is around the house. You start to notice that it is a rare occasion when everyone does something together.

One thing that parents seem to do without fail during these times is they stop talking to their children about what is going on. They do this because they want to "protect you" from the stress that they are suffering. They hope that they can work it out and that you will never know that there was even a problem. In many cases, only one of the parents wants to separate and the one who doesn't can be very upset. He or she might get depressed or angry. Some parents start spoiling the kids. Or they suddenly start trying to do all kinds of extra things with you. But, for some reason, they never sit down and tell you what is going on.

So you start feeling like that kid who is sent out of the class. You start to think it's your fault. Your parents must be talking about you. They must be upset with you. You must be causing a problem and it is so bad that your mom and dad may have to split up.

Wrong! As I said at the beginning, it's not your fault. Something else is causing the problem in your parents' marriage or relationship and they don't want you to know what it is.

So now you're wondering, what is it that is causing the problem? If it's not you, then what is it?

WHAT REALLY CAUSES DIVORCE: AT LAST THE SECRET CAN BE TOLD!

The secret? OK, I will just blurt it out, adults cause divorce! Lots of things cause parents to split up, but they do it themselves, without any help from you. Later on we will be looking at the legal reasons to get a divorce — known as the grounds for divorce — but right now I would like to examine the most common reasons for divorce to happen.

Reason 1: People Change

The most common reason for divorce is that the people who got married to each other five, ten or 20 years ago, change. Or at least one of them changes. When your parents met, fell in love and decided to marry, it was because each felt the other was a certain special person. They made each other laugh or they loved the same kind of work or they found each other really sexy. There are lots of people who get married and their friends cannot figure out why. They do not seem to get along and they are not suited to each other, but they stay together and eventually get married. Then, when they start talking about getting a divorce, everybody says "Oh, we knew it would happen sooner or later...."

The point here is not to understand all the reasons people get together but to understand that there can be certain "magical" combinations that just seem to work. I guess there are as many combinations as there are couples. If the combination of the couple changes then the "magic" that holds the couple together may be at risk. This does not mean that if you fall in love with somebody you must stay exactly the same or risk losing them. A good relationship allows the people in it to grow and change. That is what makes a relationship valuable and worth working at over many years.

Sometimes, however, one or both people in the marriage change so much or so quickly that the reason to be married and the love upon which the marriage was based simply disappears. Whoosh! Gone. All of this is not immediately obvious to your parents, the husband and wife or common-law partners. They end up thinking a lot about whether the current problem is only a rough time in the marriage — a growing experience — or whether it really is a big change that means it's over. Sometimes the rough time turns out to be a growing experience. A false alarm. Whew! No wonder they don't tell you anything. They don't want you to worry about it until they have figured out which one it is. This kind of wondering can go on for a very long time, which makes it tough on everyone, including you.

Incidentally, just because a husband and wife decide to end a marriage or to stop living together does not mean that they don't love each other. Many couples find that even though the marriage or partnership is over they still have a deep but different kind of love for each other. I have heard many parents say that, as angry as they may have gotten at the other parent, they still love the other parent because they have a child together whom they both love. Their love and caring for you never disappears. In a way it unites every mother and father. Just as I have never seen a child cause a divorce, *I have never seen parents stop loving their child after a divorce. Not once.*

Reason 2: Money

I am sure that you have heard the current complaints: "the economy is terrible" or "unemployment is high" and so on. For families, this boils down to less money coming in to meet all the expenses. In most Canadian families both parents work. They may not work full time, but they work. If one of your parents loses his or her job then the family frequently ends up under a lot of strain. Of course, some parents run their own business. If the economy slows down and other people cannot afford to buy whatever your parent sells, then the business suffers and your family can have very serious money problems.

Think of the following example: Let's say your dad loses his job because the factory he works at closes and moves to another country. He comes home and tells the family the bad news and then starts looking for a new job.

Since your family has less money to work with, your dad decides that he will definitely not buy a new car this year, or even may have to sell the one he has. Your mom may decide that she will not update some computer software that she needs or maybe replace the washer, and she may not take a planned trip to visit her family in B.C. All of those decisions affect other families because, if no one buys cars, then jobs are lost. If no one replaces computer software or washers, then department stores do not need employees to sell them. If no one takes trips, then airlines do not sell tickets and cabs do not have passengers and restaurants do not have customers. This is what people mean by "recession" or "economic downturn."

A recession can put a strain on a lot of families — not just yours. In some cases the hard times can make a family pull together. But in other families it breaks them apart. Again, there is very little that you can do about this.

Once I met a young kid named Jordan. His parents were going through a rough time. He said he never knew from one week to the next whether the family would stay together. His dad would disappear for long stretches and his mom would get really depressed. It was pretty obvious to him that money was tight for the family. He also noticed that many of his parents' arguments started about the lack of money. One day he needed $6 so he could go on a school trip to the museum. He was worried about not having the money, so he thought up his own solution. He stole it from a friend's knapsack! Eventually Jordan was caught, the principal was called and his parents were terribly shocked. None of this made the family's financial situation any better — only worse.

Your parents have the job of looking after the family financially, so let them do it. You should understand that sometimes financial problems cause stress on everyone in the family, which sometimes leads to parents separating.

Just so you don't get the idea that it is only too little money that leads to problems, I have also seen parents with problems because they have too much money. I know, I can hear you — *"Too much* money? I don't think so!" But it happens. Parents get caught up in their jobs, the money and the travel and don't have time for each other. I saw one family that got into a lot of difficulty because the father and mother suddenly came into quite a bit of money and started to spend like crazy. The money was gone pretty fast — and so was their marriage.

Reason 3: Illness

This may come as a surprise to you, but there are parents who split up because one of them gets sick. When parents get married they promise to love each other "in sickness and in health" but sometimes there is a limit to what one partner can cope with or tolerate.

Illness includes many things; it can mean a disease like cancer or it can mean being an alcoholic. Illness can be an addiction to drugs, like cocaine or crack. If a parent is addicted to alcohol or drugs or even to gambling, it may be too much for the other parent to tolerate. The other parent may feel that he or she needs to end the marriage in order to protect the children and, perhaps, themselves.

There was a story in the newspaper once about a father who took his little kids with him when he went to sell drugs. The kids didn't know what he was doing; they were just sitting in the back seat of the car. All of a sudden, a guy who was buying the drugs pulled out a gun and shot the father! The bullet went right through him and hit the little girl while she sat playing! Not many moms would want to stay with a man who did something like that.

The same thing applies to alcohol. A parent can get so drunk that he or she is a danger to the whole family. The alcoholic parent may start fights or fall asleep smoking or crash the family car. Who would want to stay with someone who did that?

I have seen parents who are addicted to gambling. They lose all the family's money betting on horses or sports or playing cards. It would be hard to live with someone who loses the family's money to satisfy an addiction.

I have seen a case where a wife developed a mental illness. She could not cope with the stress in her life and had a nervous breakdown. There were times when she heard voices in her head and when she was a danger to herself. She was often suicidal. The husband didn't know what to do. He talked to doctors and other professionals but couldn't solve the problem. They eventually separated, but the husband kept trying to get some help for the wife.

Illness may also be "addiction to ideas," for example, joining a cult. What the heck is that? That is where people get so wrapped up in a group and what it does that they forget everything but the group. I have worked on cases where mothers or fathers got involved in a "church" and could not think of anything but that group of people. They gave most of their money to the group. Sometimes they insisted that the whole family get involved. If only one parent gets involved in the cult or idea then the other partner may have a very hard time staying in the marriage.

Reason 4: New Love

I had trouble deciding whether to make this a separate category or to put it under Reason 1: People Change. What do I mean by the phrase "new love"? It's when someone new comes into your mom's or your dad's life and all those feelings that they had for each other when they got married they suddenly feel for the new person.

Wait a minute! That's not allowed, right? Once you get married, that's it. You are supposed to stay in love with that person and never fall in love with anybody new.

I wish it could be that simple. For many couples it is. They meet a special person and that is their relationship for life. The couple may have their ups and downs, they change, they adjust, they work at being married and then all of a sudden they realize that they have been married for a lifetime!

For other people it is not that simple. They fell in love, maybe they lived together for a while, and then they got married. They expected that it would last forever. You were born, brothers and sisters may have come along and then all of a sudden — new love?

I put a question mark beside the phrase because it is by no means certain that new love is also "true" love. Only time will tell. While I was writing this chapter, a guy I used to work with called me to say that, after leaving his wife for a new love two years ago, he was going back to be with his wife. The new love just didn't work out over time. I have seen other couples struggle with the arrival of a new love for months or years. It can happen to either a husband or a wife so don't think anyone is immune.

I was tempted to put this in the section dealing with change because the reason for the divorce often is not the new love; it is the underlying change in the person or the relationship. The new love often comes along after the involved parent has changed. The new person doesn't cause anything to happen. I mention this because there is a tendency to blame the new person for any trouble in the marriage. Often, that's just not fair.

Many things cause divorce in Canadian families: people change, they have financial problems, they get sick and they meet and fall in love with new people. That's the truth — not very shocking, but true.

3 WHAT YOUR PARENTS ARE GOING THROUGH: It Can Be a Little Nuts

One of the most difficult things to deal with when your parents are separating or even thinking about separating is the wild moods that they will go through. It is like the ocean — one day it is calm, the next day huge waves are crashing down on you. One day your parents are quiet and seem depressed, the next day they are unusually happy. Then, all of a sudden, they are red-hot angry about something.

How are you supposed to cope with all this craziness going on around you? Some kids are tempted to avoid it; they find any excuse to stay away from home. Other kids do the opposite; they stick to their parents — or at least one of them — like glue. Neither of these approaches is perfect because you can't really run away from the problems at home and you can't stick to your parents all the time.

So what should you do?

Well, I think it would help if you knew something about what your parents are going through. Maybe if you understood a little bit about what your parents are feeling you might learn to "surf the waves" that are suddenly all around you — instead of drowning.

I have noticed that parents who are separating and thinking about a divorce usually go through five phases. They can go through them one after the other, as I have listed them below, but sometimes they jump around a lot. So when you read this section keep that in mind.

The five phases are:

1. denial,

2. anger,

3. depression,

4. false bargaining, and

5. acceptance.

Let's look at each one. I bet some of this will sound a little familiar.

DENIAL: "THIS IS NOT HAPPENING"

To deny something is to refuse to admit that it is true. Denial can also include refusing to admit that something is happening to you. Some parents refuse to admit that they have a problem in their marriage or their relationship. This is not because they are stupid or just don't get it. Denial is caused by a lot of things. For example, it may be too painful to admit that something so serious is wrong. If your parents are really going to separate, it is going to cause major problems for them, for you, for the family. So they convince themselves that it must be something else that is causing the problem. Your mom may blame it on your dad's job (or lack of a job); your dad may blame it on your mom always being tired or not feeling well. They may take short trips alone just to have some time to themselves and to work on the problems in their relationship.

Hold it a minute!

This does not mean that every time your mom is tired or angry or your dad is late from work that your parents are getting a divorce. These things are also part of normal life. Couples fight and sulk and make up and do crazy things and still stay married. But sometimes they refuse to admit that they have a problem. In their hearts they know, but it's hard to admit it, especially to their children.

It is important for you to know about this "denial" because you may not notice anything unusual in how your parents are acting. Even if you do, your mother or father may have an excuse to shield you from what is really going on. You need to know that some-times the adults are going to pretend that everything is fine. It won't matter that your aunt or grandfather is telling them that they need to think seriously about changes to the relationship. They just deny that anything is wrong. Then, all of a sudden, the next mood hits like a giant wave...ANGER!

ANGER: IT *IS* HAPPENING AND I *HATE* THIS!

When marriages are in trouble there can be an awful lot of anger. Sometimes one parent does not want a separation to happen. That partner thinks that with some effort and cooperation the problems can be worked out. That's good. Parents should try to work things out. Important decisions should be made carefully. But just as it takes two people to get married, it takes two people to stay mar-ried. There can be a major source of anger if one parent wants to separate and the other does not. Or even worse, parents keep changing their minds! One day they think they should split, then they think they should give it another try. It is a big decision so they sometimes think twice (or more) about it. This can be very confusing for everyone, especially you, and it can make both your parents angry.

Another reason that parents can get angry is simple embarrass-ment. They often feel foolish once they realize that they have been denying problems in the marriage. One of your parents may have done something that really hurt the other parent. Maybe your father met someone new and your mother is hurt. Maybe it was your mother who met someone new and your father is angry. Sometimes, new love happens for both husbands and wives. The kids just get caught in the middle.

I will never forget one case in which the parents and kids went through some very rough times. The parents were angry for months at a time, and the kids were feeling pretty stressed out. Every time they asked their parents what was wrong and what was going to happen next, the parents would get this kind of phoney cheerfulness. "Oh, there's nothing wrong. We're just cranky these days. La la la..."

"Yeah, right," the kids thought. They knew better, but for months the parents kept up the cheerful front. Then one day the mom and dad, in a really serious mood, sat the kids down for a "family meeting." Guess what? There was a problem and it had been around for a long time. The dad had a new girlfriend and he was going to move in with her. He reassured the kids that this was not a big deal and that they would be seeing him — and his new girlfriend — regularly. The kids took one look at their mom and could see how she felt. No wonder she had been so angry! The kids were in shock ...and so was the dad after they let him have it. They were incredibly angry at their dad for lying to them, for lying to their mom and for covering things up.

For lawyers, this period of anger can be a tricky time because it may be when we first meet your mother or father. The lawyer may be working in his or her office and, all of a sudden, the telephone rings and an angry person is asking if he or she can hire the lawyer for a divorce.

When the lawyer first meets the client he or she must be careful not to do things just because the client is angry. The lawyer has to let the client calm down a little because sometimes a crisis blows over and things can be settled. But sometimes people stay angry for a long time, even after the whole process of divorce is finished.

You have to be patient with your parents and understand that this anger is natural and sometimes actually helps your parents to deal with their feelings. It is only unhealthy if they try to hurt someone or themselves, or if it keeps them from getting on with their lives. Give them lots of space, if you can, and remember — they are not angry with you. If you feel that they are taking their anger out on you (you know, like when your mom or dad blows up over some small thing like you being on the phone when she or he is waiting for a call), talk to both of them about it or talk to your other parent or get someone you trust to speak to them on your behalf. Remember your parents are not angry with you, they are angry with each other or they are angry with themselves.

You will be tempted to try to fix what you think is the problem. You may imagine that if you are extra good or if you do things a certain way then no one will be angry. Presto! The family will be saved.

Sorry. Nice try, but there is nothing that you can do to fix their problem. First of all, you may not even know what the real problem is. For instance, the kids in the family I mentioned tried everything to make their parents happy. They were always joking around trying to cheer them up. One of the kids told me he felt like a clown. His "job" was to cheer up his mom. He told me, "Sometimes I don't feel funny! I can't cheer her up. I'm letting her down..." But nothing worked for long anyway. Well, no wonder! They didn't know about the real problem in their parents' marriage. How could they fix that with a few jokes?

Second, even if you know what the problem is, it is not your responsibility to try to solve it. The adults made the problem, the adults have to fix it. When you are older you will have a crack at lots of problems — your own!

DEPRESSION: OH...THIS IS AWFUL...

Sometimes, after your mother or father has been angry, she or he may become very sad. This sadness can be very deep and make it almost impossible for them to do anything. They may not even want to get out of bed. Everything seems awful. They realize that, after denying that there even was a problem and after being really angry, it still boils down to one thing — the marriage seems to be over. This means that a lot of hopes and dreams that they shared as a couple will be lost. A big piece of their past is slipping away. At the same time, the future seems to be full of uncertainty. All the things that they thought they would be doing together suddenly will never happen. This includes raising you! Parenting together is one of the things that your mother and father planned to do for a long time and now, suddenly, it looks like it is ruined. No wonder they get depressed!

Your mother and father will need lots of support during this time. Sometimes they need the help of professionals: doctors, therapists, counsellors and psychiatrists. That is good, and often necessary to get through the period of depression. If they are lucky enough to have friends that they can lean on, then even better.

They may even lean on you for support. The person they used to lean on is gone and they love you, so it feels natural to want you around a lot. That is great too. But you are not there to save your mom or dad from their depression or anger. You are not responsible for the problems they are facing, and you are not responsible for the solutions. You are just a kid, even if you're 15 or 20 years old. Don't forget that. As I said before, I have seen kids who think they can somehow save the whole family or save the parent who is having so much trouble with the separation. These kids do it because they want to help, and no one can criticize them for that. But it is not *their* job to save the family and they probably can't do it anyway. The adults caused the problem, so the adults should fix it. Remember that.

FALSE BARGAINING: I WILL DO ANYTHING IF YOU WILL JUST STAY

At a certain point, one of your parents may decide that he or she has had enough of all the trouble that has been going on. He or she may even want to get back together with the other parent or may even want to just give up. In one case that I worked on, the father started saying things like, "I don't give a damn. Take everything. I'll just quit my job. What's the use...." He was ready to give up because the mother had decided once and for all that it was over. They had gone back and forth, apart and together, fighting and reconciling. Now, when it was finally over the father realized that he might have to sell a cottage that had been in the family for many years. For a while he stopped thinking clearly. I think he really just wanted to run away.

Just as unrealistically, one of your parents may say, "Take me back! I will do whatever you say. You were right." In one case, the mother began promising the father all kinds of crazy stuff that he did not even want. At one meeting she said, "Honey, we can take an expensive vacation — it will be a second honeymoon — maybe we can buy that new car that you have always wanted or renovate the house! Whatever you want...." Wow! The father had this puzzled look on his face as if to say, "Who is this person? I want a divorce and she wants another honeymoon?" If this happens in your family, it may sound strange to you. And it is. One minute your parents are telling each other to get lost; the next minute they're begging each other to stay or making wild promises that they probably can't keep.

This phase is what lawyers call false bargaining. The desperate parent is not trying to do these things because he or she is satisfied with the marriage, it's being done for some other motive. For example, one parent may feel guilty about what has happened and will say anything to make the problem disappear. Of course it doesn't work because, sooner or later, they both realize that the suggestion was made for the wrong reasons. Ultimately, the problem starts all over again.

You have to be careful not to get your hopes up during this phase of false bargaining. The adults are on a bit of a roller-coaster ride, and you can get dragged along whether you like it or not. So, be careful about promises or statements that seem a little unreal. It could just be a little false bargaining.

By now you are probably wondering whether it ever stops. Does the bickering and bargaining ever end? Yes, it does, and usually when both parents get to the last phase, acceptance.

ACCEPTANCE: I NEED TO GET ON WITH MY LIFE

This is the easiest phase to explain. At a certain point your mother and father will realize "Hey, there is more to life than this fight...I've got things I need to do!" Suddenly everything seems a lot clearer. Your parents may even laugh at themselves and the way they have been behaving. They may realize that they were depressed and stuck in neutral for months or years. All the crazy promises stop. They decide to deal with the real problem — the need to end the marriage and find a way to keep on being a good parent.

Unfortunately, your parents may not come to this brilliant conclusion at the same time. One of them may be ready to end the fight months ahead of the other, but he or she must wait for the other one to catch up.

When everyone accepts that it is time to move on, that the marriage is over, that it is time to do what is best for the kids, then the real problems can be solved. The lawyers are often surprised at how everything starts to move along smoothly once the phase of acceptance is reached. You will notice that your parents are much more relaxed with each other. Little things no longer get blown out of proportion. There is more cooperation and less friction, more time to focus on the kids, on work and the rest of life. I only wish couples could get to this acceptance phase sooner.

One of the most interesting cases I ever had involved a husband and wife who had waged a battle ever since the day they split up.

They were so angry with each other they could not sit in the same room. Each of them was a good parent and had no trouble looking after their two kids, a boy who was 9 and his older sister who was 12. But the minute they started to talk to each other, the fireworks would start.

As lawyers, we were being well paid (I think between the two of them they had spent about $60,000) to watch the fireworks, but nothing worked to conclude the divorce. Each lawyer looked for a way to solve the problems, but without success. Each made reasonable offers to settle the case, but none were ever accepted. Both lawyers had almost given up and were thinking that the divorce was headed for a very expensive court case. My client, the wife, had gone skiing for the weekend with the children. I planned to discuss the court case with her when she got back. Monday morning she arrived in my office without an appointment and with a very determined look on her face. I thought, "Oh no! She really wants to fight now." But I was wrong, she was determined to settle the case and move on.

I couldn't believe her change of attitude. I asked her what had happened. She said, "Michael, I was stuck on the chairlift for 20 minutes with a woman who told me about her divorce. She kept complaining about her lawyer and her husband and the courts. Her kids were depressed and her whole life was on hold until the divorce was over. She sounded like she wanted the fight to continue forever. Anyway, I told her that she should stop arguing. Life is short. Move on and enjoy your life." With a big smile she said, "I am going to take my own advice. I want to get on with life!"

We settled that case. It was fair, and the whole family seemed to let out a big sigh of relief. It is great when people accept what has happened and move on to the rest of their lives.

So, the things I've been trying to get across in this chapter are:

1. It is not your fault that your parents are going through all these moods or phases.

2. It is not your job to save the family.

You have absolutely no control over any of this, so you will just have to be patient and understanding.

And you know what? They're your parents. You gotta love 'em!

MARRIAGE, SEPARATION AND DIVORCE: Start to Finish

MARRIAGE

I guess, in order to understand what it means to get a divorce, we should start with understanding what it means to get married. Some of you probably think that talking about marriage is a waste of time. You know what a marriage is, right? Two people, a man and a woman, all dressed up, staring into each other's eyes and making some incredible promises to each other. That is the image that most people have and, for the most part, it is very true. But there are some other things about marriage that you might be interested in...so read on.

Did you know that someone did a survey of teenagers and found about 86 percent of them thought that they would get married and stay that way for life? Considering that many of those kids' parents probably got divorced, and considering that everybody talks as if divorce is so common, that is a pretty amazing amount of confidence in marriage.

If you looked at the percentage of marriages that break down, what do you think it would be — 60 percent?, 50 percent?, 35 percent?, 30 percent?, 28 percent?, or 20 percent? The correct answer is 28 percent. Not as bad as you thought, I suspect. In the United

States, the figure is a lot closer to 50 percent. We hear about U.S. statistics on TV so often, we think it is the same here. But, as you can see, Canadians do not divorce as much as Americans, though 28 percent is still a lot of divorces, and certainly a much higher rate than it was a generation ago.

In Canada people are permitted to get married only by following the marriage laws. The laws that allow marriage are passed both by the federal government, in Ottawa, and by the provincial governments. Under the *Constitution Act, 1867*, the federal level of government, through Parliament, has power over the laws of "marriage and divorce." The provinces have power over something called the "solemnization of marriage." To have a valid marriage the people involved must do what both the federal and provincial rules say.

The federal laws, for example, set the rule that one man may marry only one woman, so bigamy is a federal offence. They also say that marriage has to be "on consent." A person cannot be forced or threatened into a marriage. If a couple do not understand what marriage is, or if a person is tricked into a marriage, then the marriage will not be valid. Also, if a person is too young, then the marriage will not be legal.

The provincial laws, on the other hand, set the formal rules for the marriage itself, so each province has rules about who may perform marriages. For example, most religions perform their own wedding ceremonies and these ceremonies are perfectly legal. The provincial laws also say whether the people who want to get married need a marriage licence and, if they do, where to go to get it. The laws also say who is entitled to obtain a marriage licence. For instance, you couldn't get a marriage licence to marry your sister or your uncle, but you could to marry your second cousin. Each provincial law also says that a minor (meaning someone under the age of majority for that province) cannot get a marriage licence unless his or her parents agree. In Ontario, these and many other rules are provided for by a law called the *Marriage Act*. Every province has a similar Act.

So, when you boil this all down, what it takes to have a valid marriage is a man and a woman

- who are not married to anyone else (either they are single or divorced),
- who are of the age of majority (not a minor),

- who are consenting to the marriage,

- who are not confused or have not been tricked into getting married,

- who have followed the provincial rules and obtained a licence,

- who have had the ceremony performed by someone who is authorized by the province to perform marriages,

- who are not related to each other by blood, and

- who are able to consummate the marriage.

Consummate? What's that? It means to have sexual intercourse. If a man got married and then found out that the woman he had married could not have sex, he would be allowed to call the marriage off (a woman would also be allowed to call off her marriage to a man). When someone does that, it is called getting an "annulment" or a decree of nullity.

ANNULMENTS

Before we look at separation and divorce, let's look at annulment, because it comes up from time to time. A divorce, as we will see, puts an end to a valid marriage. An annulment is a declaration by a judge that there *never was a valid marriage*. Aside from the inability to have sex, there are other reasons for a judge to give an annulment. For example, if it turned out that one of the people getting married was already married to someone else (and never got divorced), then the marriage could be annulled. Or, if it turned out someone was mentally ill and didn't know what was going on when the wedding ceremony took place, then the marriage could be annulled.

Some religions also have a procedure for annulling a marriage. In some cases, people who want the annulments will get them from their church *and* from a judge. Catholics often ask for an annulment at the same time that they get their divorce so that later they are able to marry again within the Catholic Church. The church annuls the religious marriage and the judge dissolves the legal marriage.

The Jewish religion has a procedure known as a "get." Jews treat their religious marriages as if they were contracts. If the marriage is over, then a release from the contract is needed. The release is obtained by the man giving his wife the "get." Only the man can give it for traditional religious reasons. Once it has been given, both ex-husband and ex-wife are free to remarry within the Jewish faith. If it is not given, they cannot remarry to another Jew.

SEPARATION

Before I explain the legal aspects of separation, let's start with what parents usually do. First, they spend all their time trying to keep marital problems secret. Usually, they do a very poor job of this, so the kids start to pick up little clues that something is wrong. The second thing that many parents do is lie when their children ask about the marriage. How many of you have said, "Mom/Dad, are you getting a divorce?" or "What's going on? You're fighting all the time!" Just when you wish one of them would give you a straight answer they say, "Don't worry, we're just having a discussion...everything is fine...uh...have you finished your homework?" (Translation: Let's change the subject.) Or worse than no answer, your mom or dad starts dumping all over the other parent. Boom! "Sorry I asked," you say.

In either case, the next thing you know your father is living at grandma's house or in an apartment or with "a friend." Your mother may say something like, "Oh, your dad and I are taking a little break from each other...we need some time apart...to think...about what we want..." (Translation: We are probably getting separated but I don't know how to tell you.) Neither parent gives a straight answer until the lawyers start writing letters, or worse, when they go to court.

If only there was a good way to tell the kids that the marriage is not working, that the mother and father have decided to separate, that a good plan has been developed, that it's not the kids' fault, that both parents still love them, that they will always be involved in the lives of the kids...Hey, wait a minute! That's not so tough. So why don't parents explain it like I just did? Well, sometimes parents are so angry or hurt or shaken by the separation they just lose their balance.

What *should* parents do? They should not delay telling the children. The sooner everybody knows what is going on the better. It doesn't necessarily mean that both parents need to sit down with the children at the same time — sometimes that is not possible. If it is possible, then it should be done. The parents need to work that out in advance.

While the parents are figuring out whether they will both sit down with the children at the same time, they should also decide whether it is best to talk to all the children at once. Depending on the age and personalities of the children, the parents may want to meet them either one by one or together as a group. If possible, a group/family meeting is best. Your parents may even want to break it up into a few short discussions.

The parents should pick a good place and a time when there will be no interruptions — no one needs to rush off to hockey practice or to answer the telephone.

Once they have the place and the time, what are they going to say? Let's hope they thought about this before they sat down with you. They should be, above all else, honest. They don't need to sugarcoat the truth. Life for the next few months will probably be unpleasant. Your parents would do you a favour by explaining what is going on, and what will happen next, without being phoney.

They should be brief and to the point. If after two or three minutes you still have no idea why they asked you to sit down, be patient. Nerves can make it tough for them. Remember, they don't like this any more than you do.

If they are handling things well, they should be telling you, plain and simple, what I told you at the outset: *It isn't your fault.* They should not waste any time criticizing or blaming one another. There will be plenty of time for that later — when they are alone. Bitterness has no place in *this* discussion. I also hope that they remember to mention the fact that their marriage wasn't all bad. All marriages have good times, and it doesn't hurt to remember that during this discussion.

The other point that both parents need to make is that the separation and divorce does not mean that they are no longer parents. Divorce ends the marriage, not the job of parent. I hope they explain that they will both be around as much as possible and that they still love you.

If after all of this they start saying something like, "I'm glad we had this little talk..." and act like the meeting is over, then don't forget to say, "Hang on a second here, I have a few questions..."

Ask them anything that you need to know. Or, you may want to just say that you want some time to think about all this and that you will be back with questions. Ask questions — it helps.

That is the emotional side of the separation. Now let's look at the legal side. The fact is that one of your parents will probably relocate to a nearby apartment or go to live with his or her parents. But what about the "legal separation"? In a way, there is no such thing as an illegal separation. Once a husband and wife decide that the marriage is over and one of them moves out, they are considered, by law, to be separated.

So, what are people talking about when they say, "Sue and Jack are legally separated"? They are probably referring to the fact that, once a couple is physically separated, they often go to see lawyers who help them to negotiate a temporary settlement to the things that they may be arguing about. This settlement often outlines custody, support or property division. If parents reach an agreement on some or all of those things, the lawyers may put the details in a contract called a separation agreement. It is that agreement that people often refer to as the "legal separation." One final point: just because your parents have not signed a separation agreement does not mean that they are "illegally separated." The agreement just makes it official.

In the upcoming chapters we will look at those options for custody, access, support and some other things. Your parents may even start talking about that stuff right at the start. So sit tight, we will get to that soon. For now, let's look at...

DIVORCE

So, your parents are getting a divorce. Like tens of thousands of Canadians every year, they have decided that they — and you — would be happier if the marriage did not continue. Your parents will ask the judge to make an order that their valid marriage is over, dissolved, ended. (In Canada, divorce cases never go to a jury.) The judge acknowledges that your parents were indeed married legally but that, by order of the court, the marriage is ended. The paperwork is not particularly fancy. I put a copy of a divorce judgment in the Appendices. Take a look.

You may find this hard to believe but the actual divorce is the easiest part of the whole process. It seems to be everything else that gets parents arguing with each other — custody, access, support and division of property — that's where the fighting starts.

In Chapter 2 we looked at the emotional and other reasons for parents to split up, but what are the legal reasons — the reasons a judge wants to hear when making a divorce order?

The law of divorce is the same across Canada. The people in P.E.I. get divorced the same way as the people in B.C. The paperwork and the names of the courts may change a little, but the law that they apply is the same because the *Divorce Act* is a federal law.

The *Divorce Act* says that for a judge to order that a marriage is over there must be "grounds" for the divorce. Grounds means a legal reason. In Canada, there is one legal reason for divorce — "marriage breakdown." Seems to go in a circle, doesn't it?

A judge will agree that there has been a marriage breakdown if one of the following three things can be proved:

1. The husband and wife have lived separate and apart for one year or longer.

2. The husband or the wife has committed adultery.

3. The husband or the wife has made the other person suffer through physical or mental cruelty.

Let's look at each of these in turn.

ONE-YEAR SEPARATION

One-year separation is probably the easiest ground or reason for divorce and is by far the most popular for Canadians (about 83 percent of divorces use this ground). Your parents must live apart for 12 months because there were difficulties in the marriage. No one needs to be blamed for the decision to live apart. If they can prove to the judge that they have been apart for the 12 months, then the judge will give them the divorce.

Separated usually means not living together but, in some cases, the judge has said that the couple were "separated" even though they still lived in the same house together. If one of the people

could not afford to move out and they agreed to have separate bed-
rooms and basically lived separate lives, then that may be enough
to prove marriage breakdown.

Your parents do not need to wait until the full 12 months have
passed before they start the paperwork. Once they separate, one of
them can go to the court office (usually with a lawyer) and start
the divorce. The judge will not make the order of divorce until 12
months have passed but either the husband or the wife can start it
moving along the track. It doesn't matter who left whom, or who
was the cause of the problems in the case of a one-year separation.

Adultery

It is not that easy where the ground for the divorce is adultery.
Adultery? The word gets thrown around a lot, but what does it
mean legally? It means this: after getting married, a person has
sex with a person other than the one he or she married. Simple,
eh? Almost. Let's look at the details a little.

First, people who can prove that their husbands or wives had
sex with someone else after marriage (what people do *before* the
marriage doesn't matter) do not have to wait for a year to pass,
they can get a divorce immediately. To prove that the other spouse
committed adultery, the husband or wife must have evidence and
make an appointment with a judge to get the evidence heard.
Lawyers often get involved and the process can be very slow. How
slow? So slow that some people decide that they might as well wait
a year and get a divorce the easier way.

Also, only the person who did not commit the adultery can ask
for the divorce. If a husband starts having sex with a new girlfriend,
he cannot use his own adultery to get a divorce from his wife.
Only *his wife* can ask for the divorce. If she decides to forgive him
and stay married, then there will be no divorce on the grounds of
adultery. That adultery, incidentally, must be with a member of the
opposite sex. If a person becomes involved with a person of the
same sex (gay or lesbian) that would not be adultery.

Physical Or Mental Cruelty

The third ground for divorce — physical or mental cruelty — is
used when a husband or wife can prove to a judge that the other

partner has been so cruel that the marriage cannot continue. If it is proved, the judge will grant a divorce right away. Your mom or dad would not have to wait a year. The cruelty can be physical or mental, but it must be so bad that it would be impossible to tolerate it. That usually means that your parents are not living together.

What does it mean to be cruel? It can vary from person to person. The cruelty can be physical or mental, intended or unintended. If a person is an alcoholic and is mean when drunk, that could qualify. Mental cruelty could vary from case to case, but physical cruelty is fairly easy to understand. Punching, kicking, hitting, biting, dragging someone by the hair and threatening are all examples of physical cruelty.

These grounds for divorce apply to any marriage regardless of where it took place in the world — the United States, India, Australia, China — anywhere. As long as the person asking for the divorce has lived in Canada for at least one year before the divorce was started, the Canadian court will grant the divorce.

GETTING BACK TOGETHER

Lawyers are obliged by law to make sure that their clients really want a divorce. Like you, we would rather see a successful marriage than a successful divorce. We always ask people once they are in the office, "Is there any chance of a reconciliation?" They usually say, "Huh?" and then we ask, "You know, any chance that you two might get back together?" and then they say, "Why didn't you say so...Absolutely not!" Usually they don't get back together, but we try to encourage people to work things out if they can.

The law allows people who have separated to get back together for up to 90 days without interrupting the 12 months of separation needed to get a divorce. So a couple could separate, then get back together for a month, separate again, then get back together again for another month, separate again...and still get a divorce based on a 12-month separation. They can try reconciliation up to a total of 90 days before they need to start the 12 months of separation all over again.

A survey of lawyers who do a lot of family law showed that very few people use the 90-day period to try to reconcile. Even the ones who do use it do not generally get back together permanently.

Whenever parents try to reconcile, kids get all excited and begin to hope the divorce won't really happen. I wish it were so. One little guy told me that he was planning to be extra good if his mom and dad got back together. A little girl once let me know that she was going to make life miserable for her dad's new girlfriend so that her dad would still keep room for her mom to come back. As I said earlier, kids should not waste a lot of time worrying about that kind of stuff. The parents did not split up because of the kids, so they are not going to get back together because of the kids. I have heard of people who wanted to separate but decided to stay together a little longer "for the sake of the children." But I have not heard of anybody getting back together just because the kids are behaving differently. So relax. If they get back together, it is because of something they worked out. And don't get your hopes up — the odds aren't good for reconciliations to last very long.

HOW DO PARENTS GET THE DIVORCE?

As I mentioned earlier, the paperwork is not that complicated for a divorce. Custody, access and financial matters can be tricky, but the divorce itself is straightforward.

The divorce will either be opposed by one parent or be agreed to by both. This is usually referred to as "contested" or "uncontested." If it is uncontested then the court can deal with it quickly. In most provinces the judge does not even have to meet the people involved and there is no hearing in court. The judge will review the papers (called the "Petition for Divorce") in his or her office and sign the divorce if everything is in order. There is also an easy procedure that allows both people to sign the request for divorce. It is called a "Joint Petition for Divorce."

In some cases, the people involved argue about the custody/financial issues but not the divorce. It is possible for your parents to cut the divorce part off from all the other issues and get just the divorce. Then they can keep on discussing the other issues.

If the whole divorce is contested then your parents will exchange written versions of what happened. This is the kind of paperwork that seems to keep your mom, dad and the lawyers so busy. First the Petition for Divorce is drafted. The other parent reads it and then gives their version in an "Answer." They send the

Answer back to the other side. If they also want a divorce, but for different reasons, the person who sends the Answer may also send a "Counter-Petition." For example, your mom may want the divorce because of cruelty, but your dad says that is untrue. He may ask for the divorce because of one year of separation.

Once the other parent has read the Answer and Counter-Petition, he or she may have more to say! If so, your mom or dad would send a Reply. All of this paperwork is called the "pleadings." The lawyers and the judge read the pleadings to learn about the case.

If the lawyers have any questions they would like to ask the couple then they begin "discoveries." At the discoveries, the lawyers ask the husband and wife (and, in some cases, other witnesses) about the things they said in the pleadings. Everyone takes an oath and swears to tell the truth when answering the questions.

While this goes on the lawyers and the clients are negotiating about the case, trying to find a way of settling all the issues without going to court. Taking a case to court is expensive and sometimes satisfies neither side, but sometimes there's no choice. If your parents cannot settle, then they will meet with a judge. After hearing all the evidence, the judge makes a decision, which will include making an order for the end of the marriage — the divorce.

Maybe you can see why your parents are always talking about the lawyers and meetings and letters and telephone calls. This is where it gets expensive. The more that they argue, the more expensive it becomes. If all the documents are exchanged and there are discoveries, a divorce can cost thousands of dollars.

In concluding this chapter I want to tell you about a case with which I am familiar. This divorce was bad, real bad. The father, Jeff, met "someone new" (her name was Melanie). For a long time he kept it a secret from his wife, Ellen, and his four children. He was totally sure that Melanie was the woman with whom he was supposed to spend the rest of his life. What could he do? His wife and children depended on him. His wife had not done anything wrong, and the kids were fantastic. The father kept his secret for two years and was miserable. The children knew that something was wrong and one child, Adam, started to do very poorly in school. The kids kept wondering, "What's wrong with Dad?" Ellen had no idea what was wrong. The father blamed his work.

For two years this continued — the children thinking that there was no way they could please their dad. It didn't seem to matter what they did, he was preoccupied and upset. The kids thought their dad was upset with them, and that idea made them even more miserable.

Just when the situation was really bad, it got worse! The father told the wife about his girlfriend, Melanie, and said that he wanted to marry her. His wife was so shocked she could hardly speak. When she recovered her voice...Well, I think she said things that I cannot repeat here. She was so angry. But you know why? About a year earlier, when things were bad in the marriage, she had met a man named Allen who became a really good friend to her. She and Allen fell in love and he asked her to leave her husband, Jeff, and to marry him. She had thought about it but had said, "No, I married my husband and I think I should try to work it out." Allen was heartbroken and moved away. Just after that, her husband explained that he was leaving her for his girlfriend. That is what really caused the explosion.

The children were in the middle, convinced that everything was somehow their fault. They knew nothing about the other people involved.

Finally, the father moved out to live with his girlfriend. When Allen heard about this, he moved back to be with the mother, Ellen. The kids were confused because no one told them what was going on. One night the son, Adam, feeling totally frustrated, broke into about 15 cars. He smashed the windows and stole some tapes. He was arrested and had to call his parents. Let's just say that they were "a little upset."

They decided to have a family meeting but before the father, Jeff, got there, Melanie told him that she wanted to move out. She couldn't stand all the problems. Jeff was furious. He arrived at the meeting by himself. Allen was also there because he wanted to help out. Allen and Jeff got into a big fight and the police had to be called.

The mother and father then had a very long, contested divorce in which they both claimed that they should have custody of the children. The father said at one point that he would spend "every penny he had" to get custody of his children. It went on for a couple of years. Finally, after everyone had calmed down a little bit (and, I think, after they had received a few bills from their lawyers), they decided to talk to a mediator. (A mediator acts like a kind of referee and can sometimes help the parents find a way to resolve their differences.) After several meetings, Jeff and Ellen realized that they were letting their anger at each other interfere with their relationship with the children. Both were good parents. The children wanted to see both parents — whether the parents were married to each other or not. When someone finally asked the four kids what they wanted, they told the parents exactly that.

Eventually, Ellen and Jeff agreed to divorce. Ellen married Allen a couple of years later. The children lived with both parents. They lived with their mom during the week and with their dad on most weekends. Considering all the time and money wasted, it was not a bad settlement. The kids were a lot happier once they had their say and their new family set-up was in place. Just knowing that it had nothing to do with them was a huge relief.

I only wish the parents had been a little more open and honest at the beginning. It would have saved a lot of unhappiness (and money), both for the parents and for the kids. So, as you can see, the divorce only ends the marriage. It does not end the job of being a mother or a father.

Oh yeah, I bet some of you are wondering what happened to Adam after he got caught breaking into those cars. He was found guilty, but he was given an absolute discharge. That means, although he was found guilty, he will not have a criminal record. His parents paid for all the damage. Adam was quite angry with his dad for awhile, but they straightened things out and he is now doing well in school. Close call, I'd say.

5

LAWYERS, JUDGES, MEDIATORS, SOCIAL WORKERS: Who Are All These People?

Once a family starts to separate, a great many people can get involved. I thought in this chapter it might be helpful if I introduced you to the main characters and to some of the lingo that they use. We will take a brief look at lawyers, judges, mediators and another important professional who may be involved, the social worker.

LAWYERS

People seem to get a kick out of making fun of lawyers. Everybody seems to know at least one joke about lawyers that compares us to sharks or something just as bad. I think that lawyers get picked on for three reasons. First, we tend to be called up when somebody is already in trouble. We are sort of like dentists — nobody calls unless they have a toothache. Second, lawyers have a reputation for being very expensive. We make money on other people's troubles. Third, people do not think very much of lawyers when they see us helping criminals to "get off" after they have been accused of a crime. Although you may get a different impression from watching American TV shows, Canadian lawyers have a reputation around the world of being very well-trained, honest and fair.

The lawyers that I would like to look at in this section are the lawyers who represent husbands, wives, children and other family members when a family is separating or going through a divorce. In later chapters you will see that there are all kinds of problems that can come up. Many of them can be solved with the help of a good and experienced lawyer.

The first question that parents often ask is, "Do I really need a lawyer for this?" There is no law in Canada that says people must hire a lawyer when they get a divorce, when they separate, or when they start living with someone. But the problems that come up when these things happen — and the way the laws work — can make everything a little complicated. There are choices that need to be made, and people sometimes need advice on which choice is best in the circumstances. That is where lawyers come in. We are trained to understand how all the laws might apply to the different situations that people get into.

After the lawyer has a good understanding of what the facts are, he or she can then make suggestions on how to proceed. That is really what legal advice is all about: learning the facts, understanding the way the law applies to those facts and making suggestions as to what a person should do.

I always suggest that parents who have family problems learn as much as they can about the law on their own and *then* go to a lawyer for advice. If your parents read up on the law and have a basic understanding of how the system works, then they will be much better clients for any lawyer. Their knowledge will also make it easier for the lawyer to give them advice.

Lawyers call the people they are working for their "clients." Clients are the same as customers. I remember when I first started working in a law firm many years ago, we hired a young woman to work as our receptionist. She kept calling out to the lawyers, "Mike, you have a new customer waiting!" After a couple of weeks she got used to the more refined term, "client." But she was right all along. They really are customers.

Lawyers have a special relationship with the people that they advise. We call them "clients," we say that we are "acting" for them or that we "represent" them, and we are covered by special rules in our dealings with them. The rules are called the *Rules of Professional Conduct* and they are for all Canadian lawyers.

One of the most important rules for you to know concerns "confidentiality" — keeping things that people tell us a secret. When people come in to ask for a lawyer's advice, they must be confident that they can tell the lawyer *everything* — and I mean *everything*. The only way the lawyer can provide accurate advice is if he or she knows the full story. If a client thinks that the lawyer might blab the information to someone else, then he or she will not tell the full story. If that happens the advice would be fouled up and nobody would get anywhere.

So, if your mother or father hires a lawyer, he or she should be confident that anything told to the lawyer will be a secret. I know what some of you are thinking — "Anything?" There are only two things that a lawyer can reveal. First, a crime — if a client told a lawyer that he or she was going to commit a crime, then the lawyer is allowed to break the rule. If a man said that he was so upset that he was going to kill his boss at work, then the lawyer could call the police. Second, child abuse — if a parent came in to see a lawyer and mentioned, for example, that the other parent was beating or sexually abusing the children, then the lawyer could break the rule and report the abuse.

So, if a lawyer is needed, why can't both parents use the same lawyer? Because it is very important that each person have the ability to go and speak in confidence to his or her *own* lawyer. There may be things that each parent needs to tell a lawyer that they don't want the other parent to know about. The stories that the clients tell to the lawyers will be different; this means that the advice from the lawyers will be different. Lawyers call this "independent legal advice."

In a divorce, each parent sees his or her own lawyer, each lawyer listens to the story of the parent and then provides suggestions on what the parent should do. The suggestions are based on the law and how the lawyer thinks the case would be decided if it were heard by a judge. You can see how important it is for your parents to see a lawyer who is experienced in family law. If the lawyer doesn't do many family law cases, his or her advice won't be reliable.

After the lawyers have explained the choices available to the clients, they get directions from the clients on what to do next. After that, the two lawyers may start to negotiate with each other.

If the lawyers and their clients cannot agree on a way of settling the case then it may well go to court. There the judge will have to read all the facts, look at the positions of the clients and the different views of the lawyers and decide what settlement is most appropriate.

Later, we will look at some of the possible choices in more detail, but at this stage we need to be clear about the following:

• The parents should have different lawyers.

• The lawyers must be experienced.

• The clients must be totally honest with the lawyers and the lawyers must keep things they are told in confidence.

• The lawyers must provide good advice, based on the law and their experience.

• The clients must tell the lawyers what they want them to do, based on the lawyer's advice.

If your parents don't have a lawyer already, there is a simple way to get a list of local lawyers. Every province and territory in Canada has a Lawyer Referral Service. You can call the Law Society for your region and ask them to give you a list of lawyers who specialize in family law. It does not do any good to go to a lawyer because he did a great job on Uncle Fred's car accident, or because she did a terrific job on Grandma's will. Your parents need a lawyer who knows about family law.

Some provinces, like Ontario, give lawyers who specialize in family law a certificate that says they are certified as a family law specialist. Of course, that is not the only thing to look for. People should also *feel* personally comfortable with their lawyer. They should have confidence in the lawyer and feel that the lawyer respects their opinion. Your parents don't go to a lawyer so he or she can *tell* them what to do. They go for advice and for help to make decisions. Family law cases can be very emotional so parents should find a lawyer who is understanding and supportive.

The client and lawyer usually sign a written agreement (called a "retainer") to have the lawyer do certain things for the client. The retainer sets out the amount the lawyer will charge and other important details. Lawyers charge by the hour, and their fees can range from $100 an hour up to $400 an hour, depending on the lawyer and the problem. The average family law lawyer will charge about $200 to $250 an hour. When the matter is in court, legal fees can run to $2,000 a day. This is why divorce can be so expensive for some warring parents.

To earn all this money, the lawyer listens to and talks with the client, makes telephone calls, writes letters, does research, drafts court documents, meets with witnesses and goes to court. Everything is kept track of and the time is added up. If a lawyer does three hours' research, then it is multiplied by the hourly rate, say $200. Add to this the cost of photocopies, faxes and taxes, and you have the lawyer's bill.

Let's consider what might happen to one of your parents if he or she hired a lawyer. We will use your dad as an example, but the same applies for both mom and dad.

First, your dad would go to an interview to see if he felt comfortable with the lawyer. They would talk about the divorce case and how involved it might be. The lawyer would explain how much the charge would be per hour and how much work might be involved. This would just be an estimate because it is hard to predict accurately at the first meeting.

At these first meetings, I always try to get a feel for what mood the client is in. If the client is angry, I might suggest cooling off for a couple of days. I would explain my approach to such cases and review a draft retainer agreement — the legal contract that lets me represent the client.

A lawyer may also explain that, before taking the case, he or she will need some money up front. Very few lawyers will go to the trouble of starting to work for a client, opening a file and telephoning the lawyer on the other side, unless they have a good chunk of money in the bank first. This can range anywhere from $500 up to $10,000, depending on how complicated the case may be. Most lawyers like to get paid in advance. We keep the money in trust until the work has been done. Once the work is finished, we send a bill.

The total cost of a separation and divorce can be quite high. I have worked on cases where I have charged $50,000 for the work I have done. The total bill is not sent all at once. It usually is spread out over many months. Suddenly your parents may be paying an extra $500 or more each month just to cover the lawyers' fees.

You can imagine the reaction of your mother or father when a lawyer says, "Yes, Mr./Mrs. Brown, you have an excellent case and I would love to work for you. Oh, by the way...I need $10,000 up front."

"Whaaaaat?!...I...I...I don't have $10,000..."

Now you know why your parents can be a little grumpy when they get the lawyer's bills.

Some clients qualify for what is known as legal aid. Because their earnings are low or because their debts are so high, they may need some help with the lawyers' bills. It is necessary to apply for this help (look in the Yellow Pages of your telephone book) and to reveal how much you have in the bank. Not everyone gets it. There have been cutbacks lately, and some provinces are talking about not giving people legal aid for divorce cases at all.

Legal aid works like this. The lawyer agrees to reduce the fee for the case. Instead of $200 an hour, the lawyer might charge only $80. The bills are sent to the legal aid office and they send the lawyer a cheque. Clients, in many cases, sign an agreement to pay back the legal aid fund if they get some money later. The kinds of things that the lawyer is allowed to do are also limited by the legal aid fund.

Some of you may be thinking, "Why would lawyers accept $80 an hour? They probably won't work as hard for the clients." That is a fair question. Lots of lawyers refuse to take legal aid cases because it costs them more than $80 an hour to run their office. On the other hand, there are some lawyers who are happy to do it. They may be young lawyers just out of school who need experience. Other lawyers do it because it is a way of helping the public.

After the divorce is finished, if a person thinks the lawyer charged too much, or that the work wasn't worth the amount charged, then it is possible to complain at the courthouse and try to get the bill reduced. It is also possible to fire your lawyer and switch to another while the case is still going on.

On television you may have noticed that, while in court, Canadian lawyers sometimes wear fancy black gowns and special ties. (In England the lawyers even wear special white wigs to court.) These clothes are a part of the tradition of the courts and legal profession that make the Canadian system very special. American lawyers don't wear such fancy outfits.

Most family law lawyers try to do a good job for their clients for a reasonable cost. They also try to get the work done as quickly as possible. The best thing for parents to do is to take their time and find a lawyer who is experienced, honest and with whom they feel comfortable. Once they find that lawyer, they should make sure that they have a written retainer that says exactly what the lawyer will do, when it will be done and how much will be charged. If the clients also take the time to do a little work on their own before they go in to talk to the lawyer, then they will have a much easier time dealing with the problem and with the lawyer. I wrote a book called *Surviving Your Divorce* just for people who were going through this process.

While it may come as a total shock to you, sometimes kids get to have their own lawyer too. If a family law case involves custody and access and the judge wants to know what the children think, he or she may appoint a lawyer for the children. The lawyer meets with the children, discusses the case and asks what they would like to have happen. The lawyer also explains the system to the children and what the choices are.

In Ontario, these lawyers work for a part of the Attorney General's office called the "Office of the Children's Lawyer." It used to be called the Official Guardian's Office. These lawyers will not get involved in every case. In fact, they will only come in if the court orders it. Sometimes they come in just to investigate what is going on and what might be best for the children. They may even try to help the parents and the lawyers reach a settlement.

If you are worried that one of these children's lawyers might be appointed to represent you and that you are going to get a big bill, relax. They do not charge for the work. These lawyers are paid by the government. It is something like legal aid. These lawyers are often regular lawyers who do family law cases but they have had extra training on how to represent children. Whenever a judge needs someone to represent a child, one of these lawyers is called and asked if he or she wants the case.

I did some work as a children's lawyer and really enjoyed it. The pay was not great, about $50 an hour, but I thought that the children were fantastic. They knew a lot more than their parents gave them credit for. One of the toughest cases I took was representing an 8-year-old girl who had been left alone to look after herself while her mother went to Spain for three weeks. A neighbour called the police and the child protection people came and took her to a foster home until her mother got back.

I went and met with the girl after school one day. We chatted in the bedroom she was sharing with another little girl in the foster home. She was a great kid and really knew how to look after herself. She often made me laugh with her questions. She was so smart! She wanted to know if she would have to go to court. (Not unless absolutely necessary. I would relay her information to the judge.) Would it be a man or a woman judge? (Depends on which judge is sitting that day. They rotate.) When could she go home and go back to her regular school? (Depends on how quickly we can meet with her mom and other family members to find out why this happened and to make sure it would not happen again.) How much was I charging her? (Nothing.) Could she have my card to show her friends that she had her own lawyer? (I gave her a card and told her she could call me anytime.)

That young girl was smarter than a lot of adults. She told me exactly what she wanted and all the important details about her life and school. I went to court and told the judge what she had told me, and you know what? The judge agreed and ordered exactly what she wanted. I phoned to tell her the good news and sent her a letter to tell her about the case, just like I would with any client. I used to drop in on her for surprise visits every once in a while just to make sure everything was OK. She was just fine.

JUDGES

About a year ago my daughter's class and I did a pretend court hearing. This is called a "mock court." We invented a story about the robbery of a store and had a full trial with her classmates doing jury work, playing witnesses (some very good performances!) and being court clerks. We even had some of them pretend to be newspaper and TV reporters. I played the judge. We had a ball and videotaped the whole thing. At the end I said "Would anybody like to be a lawyer now?" All the kids put up their hands except for one girl in the corner. She said, "I want to be the judge!" I could understand why, because a judge has a lot of power and a very interesting job.

In order to become a judge you need to be a lawyer first. Most provinces want the lawyer to have about ten years' experience before being appointed as a judge. The expression used to describe the process is "being appointed to the bench." Many years ago, when judges became a part of our legal system, they sat on a bench up above the lawyers and their clients. That is where the expression came from. In many courtrooms this still applies — the judge sits on a platform elevated above everyone else. The judges usually are called "Your Honour" or "My Lord" or "Madam Justice." In one case a witness was a little nervous and kept calling the judge "Your Majesty." I think the judge liked it.

In court, the judge's job is to listen to the witnesses and the lawyers. Lawyers for each side will tell the judge how they think the case should be decided. The judge will take notes and watch the witnesses to see if they are being open and honest. At the end of the case, the judge writes out the decision, called a judgment.

There are several levels of judges, some more senior than others. They range all the way from Small Claims Court and Traffic Court judges right up to the Supreme Court of Canada, which deals only with appeals. An appeal is when a person asks a judge in a higher court to review the decision of another judge. Sometimes a judge makes a mistake, misunderstands a law or makes a decision that was not fair. In most cases, but not all, the people involved and their lawyers can ask for the decision to be reviewed on appeal.

Judges are paid by the government. They do not charge by the hour or the case. They are paid a salary that is, in many cases, over $100,000 a year. They work hard for the money, though, since it is not easy sitting day after day listening to all the problems people get themselves into.

If your parents' divorce goes to trial, will you get to be a witness? Do you think that would be exciting? Being a witness can be stressful and in family law cases it is pretty rare. Judges don't like to put young people in the position of looking like they are picking one parent over the other. Sometimes the judge will meet with an older child (over 12) with the lawyers present. Most of the time the lawyers and the judge try to find other ways to solve the case. For example, someone who has talked to the child may be allowed to relay the evidence to the judge. Ultimately, the judge is the one who will weigh all the evidence. In upcoming chapters we will see some of the things that judges look for in cases involving young people.

In court, judges are assisted by various people, such as court reporters, who write down everything people say in court. This is an interesting and important job because sometimes the lawyers and the judge need to go back and check to see what someone said. Court reporters write the testimony down by hand or type it on special "silent typewriters." A few reporters use something called a stenomask, which is just that — a big plastic mask into which they repeat everything for transfer to a tape recorder.

The judge also has assistants called court clerks and bailiffs. They make sure everything is ready to go and that witnesses get to and from the witness box. They also keep track of anything that is used as evidence in court.

MEDIATORS

We will look at mediation in detail in Chapter 9. At this stage, however, I thought you should know that mediators are often a big help in settling family law disputes. Mediators are objective and neutral third persons who help parents try to figure out solutions to divorce problems. They are sometimes lawyers or social workers who have been specially trained to help people discuss alternative ways of meeting everyone's interests. Mediators can be especially good in custody and access cases. They do not work just for the father or just for the mother. They work for and with both sides at the same time. Instead of making each side work against the other, they help them work together. If both parents are equal in their ability to negotiate, then mediation can work very well. It would not work if one parent is threatening the other or if there has been violence in the family.

The people who use mediators will still need to have any agreement they reach looked over by their lawyers to make sure it is fair and complete. If it is, the lawyers will have it typed up and get the parents to sign it. After that it is binding.

SOCIAL WORKERS

When family law cases involve children, social workers may become involved. Social workers are not lawyers, though they are sometimes trained to act as mediators. Their job is to help the family with non-legal problems. If a parent has trouble looking after the family because of the separation, then a social worker might come in and help with some suggestions or provide some counselling. Social workers may meet with the children to see how they are doing and will even talk to teachers if asked. They are not there to help sort out the legal issues. They are there to help with the emotional and other family problems that sometimes occur when a divorce hits a family. They may work for a Children's Aid Society (the CAS) — a community organization set up to help kids when there is a crisis in a family. For example, I have seen a case where a mother got involved with drugs, took an overdose and could not look after her child. The CAS was called and a social worker arranged for the little girl to stay in a foster home until the CAS located the grandparents who could then look after her.

All the above people — lawyers, judges, mediators and social workers — are the main players in most divorces, separations and other family cases. Now that we know a little about them, let's move on to look at custody and access in a little more detail.

6

CUSTODY AND ACCESS:
Where Am I Going to Live?

About a year ago I was a guest on a radio program. I was taking telephone calls from people with questions about divorce and family law. It was nearly 4 p.m. and we had time for only a couple more calls when a young girl named Katie called in. She was finished at school for the day, and her parents were not yet home from work. I could barely hear her voice as she explained that she was worried about her parents and herself. Her parents, she said, had been arguing. They had been talking about divorce and about one of them having to move out. She said that, in all the shouting, she had heard her parents saying something like, "What about Katie?" She wanted to know what was going to happen to her. Where would she live? Would she see both her parents again? What about her brother and sister? Would they be separated?

Pretty important questions.

I imagined her mother or father, maybe driving home from work, listening to the radio. All of a sudden they hear their daughter asking for advice on the radio! Swerve! Screech! They probably would have a million answers for her questions by the time they got home. They'd certainly feel embarrassed that they had not thought about their children's feelings and worries in all the commotion over the separation.

I think sometimes parents feel that whatever they decide will just have to suit the kids. Once they have figured out all the answers *then* they will discuss it with the kids. That may be OK for babies or really young kids, but it is no help to someone your age.

In this chapter I would like to look at all of the things that parents may need to think about when trying to figure out the very difficult question, "What to do about the kids?" I also want to look at how you kids can have a say in all of this decision making.

Let's start by admitting that custody and access are the most emotional things that parents have to decide. Both parents love their children. Neither of them can imagine not seeing you every day. It is quite common to hear both parents say, "I must have custody!" This happens for a bunch of different reasons. For example, some parents fear that other adults will think that they do not love their children unless they demand the children be with them. One parent may feel that only he or she can properly care for the kids. One of the parents may have a job that keeps him or her travelling a lot. It might not seem realistic for that parent to want the children to live with him or her, but still I have seen such people seek custody. Sadly, I have even seen cases where one parent wanted custody of the children in order to punish the other parent for breaking up the marriage and the family. In one case the father had met someone new, fallen in love and wanted to be with that new person. The mother was angry and said, "Fine, if you want to leave, then leave...but the children stay with me!"

In other cases I have seen parents get very upset when talking about children and divorce because it reminds them of their own parents' divorce or a friend's divorce that was unpleasant. Frequently, both parents are upset because they really had planned for you to be raised in a happy two-parent family and now, out of the blue, they are another statistic, another divorce. They blame themselves for "ruining your life."

So, you can see that parents have plenty of reasons to get anxious about where the children will live. The reason I mention this is so that you will understand why your parents get so emotional when they try to discuss your custody at the time of divorce. Most of the time they are just afraid that they will not have the same kind of life with you that they enjoyed before or that they hoped for in the future.

Why would they worry? Surely they should just agree to something practical. Right? You will keep seeing both of them. Right? You will keep getting advice or decisions from both of them. Right? Well, it is not always so straightforward. So let's take a look at the things that your parents are thinking about.

The two words that you will hear most often are "custody" and "access." These are the legal terms that are designed to summarize all the sharing of decision making concerning children. I bet you are probably thinking "Hmmm, I thought it had to do with living in one house with my mom and visiting in another with my dad." It could. That is a big part of custody — where you will live and when you will see the other parent. But it also involves a lot more.

Every day parents have to make all kinds of decisions about their children — or at least be prepared to make them. If the family is living together, then the mom and dad will usually (but not always) consult with each other when making decisions. In other families some things are more important to one parent than the other. For example, the father may be very concerned about decisions regarding the religious practices of the children and the mother may be more concerned about decisions regarding education. They may divide up the decisions.

At the time of separation, parents must think about decisions concerning you. These decisions include:

• where you should live,

• where you should go to school and other educational choices,

• what your extra-curricular activities (sports, hobbies) should be,

• what health decisions should be made, especially in an emergency,

• whether you should move to another city or province, or even another country,

• whether you should change your last name,

• what religion, if any, you should practice,

- whether and when you should visit the other parent, or other family members in some cases, and

- whether you can travel outside the country with the other parent.

If the parents have separated, then it can be a little tricky making some of these decisions together.

If your parents can agree to make the decisions together by sharing the parenting load, that is great. We will look at ways to do that in more detail later on. But, if they cannot agree, maybe because they are so angry at each other, they may have to get some help or have someone else make the decisions for them. Ultimately, the decisions may be left in the hands of a judge — though this is rarely the best outcome.

CUSTODY

A judge once said that custody of a child meant having the full bundle of rights to make all significant decisions about that child. These usually include decisions about health education, welfare and religion. When a parent has complete custody of a child, it is sometimes referred to as "sole custody." This means that the child lives with that parent every day and every night. When a school form asks for the name, address and telephone number of the parent, then the information given is that of the sole custodial parent. If the child is injured during gym class and an emergency medical decision has to be made, then the custodial parent makes the decision. If you switch to a new religion, same thing.

When I describe the parents in this chapter sometimes I will use the mother as the custodial parent. I want you to be very clear that either parent can be the custodial parent. There are lots of fathers out there who are looking after their children as custodial parents. If, however, you looked at the statistics you would see that most custodial parents are mothers. This happens for several different reasons. For example, it may have been the mother who stayed home from work to look after the children, and the father may have been the one who had the steady job. It was logical for them to keep on doing those jobs for the family.

Sometimes parents simply agree that one of them should have sole custody. They agree, for example, that the children will live with the mother and that she will make all the decisions. The mother may promise to consult with the father on important matters but, if there is no time, due to an emergency, or they cannot agree, she will make the decision on her own.

About ten years ago that was the way most cases were settled. The mother had sole custody and could make all the decisions about the children. The other parent, usually the father, would still want to see his children regularly, so the mother and father would often agree to "access." Other words are sometimes used to describe "access." In the United States they call it "visitation." Both words mean that the children and the non-custodial parent (let's call him or her the access parent) have a chance to spend time together on a regular basis. When parents agree, say, that the mother will have custody, they usually also agree that the father will have access on a reasonable and generous basis. So the custody/access agreement about the kids might say:

> The mother and father hereby agree that the mother will have sole custody of the children of the marriage until they reach the age of 18. The father will have liberal and generous access to the children on days and at times to be agreed upon from time to time and as may be appropriate to the needs of the child...blah blah blah...

In some cases, parents get very specific about access times and other details. I remember a divorce case involving a mother and father of two children, Beth, age 6 and Carrie, age 8. The parents were angry with one another for several months and could not agree on a way to arrange the time with the kids. Both of them were good parents and both of them had been really involved in raising the kids. The father had a very busy job and often worked until 6 p.m. weekdays. He also had a bit of a trip home on the bus after work, so sometimes he would not get home until 7 p.m. The best part of his job was that he never had to work weekends. The mother had a good job at the local library and could be home each day when the kids got home from school. The kids would do their homework and be ready for their father when he got home. But the mother had to work Saturdays at the library. Over the years they had worked out a nice routine. The kids had never really thought about it, but now that the parents were separating they wondered why they could not just keep to the same routine.

In the middle of the case, the father told me something that was very important. He had heard from a friend that he should never give up custody because the minute the mother had custody, his friend said, the father would slowly start losing his time with the children. The father really didn't trust the mother to let him stay involved with the kids.

I got into the middle of this. I said, "What if we write out exactly when you will have your time with the children? Then there can be no misunderstanding about what you and the children are entitled to."

He asked, "We can do that?"

I said, "Sure. For example, you might agree that the children will spend time with you every second weekend from Friday night at 6:30 p.m. until Sunday evening at 6:30 p.m., every Saturday from 9:00 a.m. to 5:00 p.m. and maybe alternating Wednesday evenings from 7:00 p.m. to 8:30 p.m. Alternating Wednesdays means that if it is a week in which the children will not see you on the weekend, then they will spend time with you on the Wednesday evening. If it is a week in which they will see you on the weekend, then they would not see you on the Wednesday night. That way it is alternating."

The father asked, "What about all the other times that are so important with the kids?"

"Well," I explained, "at the same time you're sorting out the day-to-day schedule you must also think ahead. What will happen on birthdays? What about religious holidays? What about summer vacations? The March break? Other special occasions in the family? Groundhog Day? Just kidding, but every family has its own special customs.) All of these dates must be considered. Some parents agree to alternate the holidays; some set out specific schedules; some figure it out one month at a time; and some argue about every single holiday."

After talking about the schedules, and his work and other stuff, we were able to make out a nice easy schedule for everyone involved, especially Beth and Carrie.

I know what you're thinking: "It must be exhausting!" It can be. But the sooner everyone understands the choices and the importance of cooperating, the sooner custody and access can be resolved. You can see why it is so important for you to understand what your parents are discussing so that you speak up about what is important to you.

Another consideration that I will mention here, briefly, is the possibility that it is not just your parents who will be competing for a slice of your time. Your grandparents, aunts, uncles, cousins and others are all able — in law — to ask for access to you. I'll give you more details on this issue later. But remember, in a separation and divorce two whole families may end up arguing!

The bottom line is that the people involved can agree to any type of arrangement that works for them. If they don't, the court will make an order for them, but it won't be nearly as flexible as an arrangement that parents could set up themselves.

Those are the basics of the way custody and access have worked in the past. Now let's take a look at how the legal decisions about custody and access are made as well as some of the newer arrangements that parents are trying, things like "joint custody" or "shared parenting."

GUIDELINES FOR CUSTODY AND ACCESS

The laws that have been put in place to help families who are separating or going through divorce provide everyone with guidelines for deciding what to do about the children. The guidelines are not complicated and actually suggest little more than using some common sense. But, with all the emotions surrounding this issue, I guess the adults sometimes need a little reminder!

What is the basic guideline? Everyone is supposed to do what is in the "best interests" of the children! I told you it wasn't complicated. This seems kind of obvious, doesn't it?

In Ontario, the provincial Parliament passed a law that sets out some of the things people should think of when trying to figure out what is in your best interests. The law is called the *Children's Law Reform Act* and every province and territory has something similar. The *Divorce Act*, which is the law for divorces across the whole country, uses the same test. So let's look at the things that parents need to be reminded about and things that the judge will be looking at.

1. *The love, affection and emotional tie between the child and the person claiming custody.* Also considered are the other members of the family who would live with the person claiming custody, or would be involved in caring for the child. So, for example, the court will want to know who is closest to you. If your mom was going to live with her parents (your grandparents) after the separation and you are close to them, then the judge would think that having you near them would be great. This is especially so when the separation is rough on the kids.

2. *The views of the child — you — if the child is mature enough to say.* Some kids have a clear preference on where and with whom they want to live. The court will want to know about it.

3. *The length of time the child has lived at the place where he or she is currently living.* Have you been with your mother for eight months since the separation? Have you been bounced around from parent to relative to day care and so on? If you have been in a stable home for a while, then the court will not want to disturb the situation. Lawyers and judges sometimes call this "preserving the status quo."

4. *The ability of the person asking for custody to provide the child with guidance, education and all the things a child needs to have a basically normal life (legally called "the necessaries of life").* Which parent can provide you with the things you will need every day — a home, food, school, medical attention, and so on. Can the parent seeking custody meet any special needs that you have (like special medical treatment for asthma or diabetes)?

5. *The plans of the person seeking custody for the care of the child.* Where will you live? What school will you go to? After school care? Brownies? Scouts? Sports and so on. What is the plan?

6. *The stability of the family with which you will live.* Which home will be more solid and dependable? For example, if, right after the separation, your dad met someone who had never had children, and they had been living together for only a week, the judge might think that that was not yet a solid relationship. The judge might not want to put you into such a situation for fear that, if it didn't work out, then you would have been through two separations.

7. *Finally, whether the child — you — is related through blood or adoption to the person claiming custody.*

When the judge or the parents consider these things, they usually focus on what is most likely to be in the child's best interests. They are not supposed to get sidetracked by who did what to whom or how awful somebody was five years ago at a New Year's Eve party. The only thing that is relevant is whether somebody can be a good parent and whether it is best for you. (And you thought they didn't care!)

You may have noticed that one of the things everybody is supposed to consider is what you think. I know what you're wondering — "You mean I get a say in the divorce?" In a way, you do. The judge would never want to make an order that the child would hate. For example, I remember a case that I was involved in a few years ago where a 13-year-old girl named Kirsten wanted to live with her dad. Her mom and dad were both great parents, but her dad had been working from a home office for the last two years. He was the one who was there when she came home from school. He was the one who took her to all her activities and appointments. And he was the one whom she wanted to keep on doing those things.

The hard part was that Kirsten's mom was hurt. The mom was very devoted to Kirsten. She had started a new career as a head-hunter (someone who finds jobs for other people) and was good at it. The mother made great money but had to travel all the time. Kirsten told anyone who would listen — her mom, her dad, the lawyers, the family and her friends — "I want to live with my dad and see my mom regularly." Kirsten's mom said she would quit her job if she had to, but that would have been unreasonable and unfair to her. Still, Kirsten's mom could not stand the thought of not seeing Kirsten whenever she wanted.

After six months the lawyers finally said to the parents, "What is the point of ordering this girl to do something she clearly does not want to do? She will just disobey the judge's order. Let's spend some time and figure out how she can see lots of her mom on short notice."

Kirsten was thrilled, "Finally someone is listening to me!" she said. She got to live with her dad and saw her mom regularly — as a matter of fact, she sees her almost as much as when the family was under one roof.

So, this raises the key question: At what age will a kid's views be considered seriously? Little toddlers can't really express an opinion. Kids who are, say 5 or 6, can speak pretty clearly, but they may not understand everything that is going on. It is only when kids are 9, 10, 11 and older that their opinions really can be helpful.

The best way to let someone know what you want is just to tell them. I know that can be hard because parents may be hurt if they think that children do not want to live with them. I put some work sheets in the back of this book (see Chapter 13) to help you work out some of this stuff. You will remember from Chapter 5 that there will be lots of adults trying to help. Both of your parents will probably have lawyers, there may be a social worker involved, the judge may want to know what you think and you may even have your own lawyer.

Be honest. If no one knows what you really want, then there is no way for them to figure out how to get it for you. You will see in the next few sections that there are several choices available.

Don't let yourself be manipulated or controlled. One of the reasons that the judges and lawyers put less emphasis on the words of very young children is out of concern that the parents may try to influence the kids. Everyone has heard the joke about the mother saying, "Oh, I know we live in a small apartment but, if you live with me you can have a pony!" or the father who says, "That's right son, I know you're only nine, but you can have a motorcycle! If you live with me that is...." Those bribes are a bit exaggerated, but it is true that parents will sometimes try to *persuade* you that it really is best if you live with them. Lawyers call this "poisoning the child's mind." Parents have their reasons for trying to coax you, but you have to think about what you really want.

Don't live with one parent just because he or she:

- makes you feel sorry for him or her,
- will be lonely,
- promised you a present or something,
- will be angry if you don't,
- has been bad-mouthing the other parent,
- will be hurt, or
- needs to be looked after.

You should probably ask to live with a parent who:

• will know how to look after you — and has actually done it,

• will keep you in touch with your friends and family — both sides, that is,

• will keep you in regular contact with the other parent — in person and by letter or phone,

• will keep as much of your current life in place as possible (for example, the same school, house, neighbourhood, friends, lessons, sports, hobbies and so on),

• will have a healthy attitude about his or her own needs, and who

• will be realistic about the changes that are going on in your lives.

When looking at custody/access situations the judge may use some general rules. For example, the judge will not want to disturb an arrangement that seems to be working. (Remember the "status quo"?) In addition, the judge will not want to split up brothers and sisters. It is very unusual for a judge to give one child to one parent and a brother or sister to the other parent. Judges will tend to keep smaller children (babies and toddlers) with the mother, especially if the children are being breast-fed.

Another tool that is sometimes used to clear up custody issues is called an "assessment." An assessment is when the lawyers and the judge think that it might be a good idea to get an outside, objective, neutral person to come in and look at the situation. That person — often a social worker — writes a report that assesses the home situation.

The person then makes recommendations to everyone about what should happen with the children. There is no requirement that the report be followed, it is just an objective person's suggestions. If a child is old enough, the assessment is a great opportunity for the child to say exactly what he or she wants. The assessor is neutral. If the assessor writes a report that says you have expressed a clear preference for living with your mother, that can be very influential with the judge.

There are no special rules for talking to the assessor, just be honest. Ask questions if you don't understand. The person may interview you only once so lay out every concern when you have the chance. Be careful that you don't let your parents' wishes creep into the discussion. The person doing the assessment will also interview your parents, and they will have their turn. Tell your side of the story.

An expression that is sometimes used in custody cases is the "friendly parent rule." Sounds odd, doesn't it? A rule that parents must be friendly? Almost. When the judge has two arguing parents in front of the bench and they cannot agree on a custody arrangement, one thing the judge will consider is which parent is most likely to cooperate with the other parent on things that affect the children. In other words, which parent is friendly to the idea of the kids seeing the other parent? If the judge orders that the children be in the legal custody of the mother, will she make it hard for them to see the father? If the judge thinks she might, then the judge may order that the father have custody. This is especially true if the father can be counted on to make sure that the kids see the mother.

If the custody order has been made or your parents have reached an agreement about what to do, it will stay like that unless something pretty drastic happens that calls for a change. This is called a "material change in circumstances." For example, if your father got a job in Australia, it would probably be hard to see him every second weekend. That would be important enough to make the judge change the first order. This is called a "variation order." No order affecting children is ever permanent. The judge always has the right to change it if ... you know ... it is in your best interests, of course!

JOINT CUSTODY

Let's take this section to look at one of the latest developments — "joint custody" (sometimes called "shared parenting" or "co-parenting").

A few of you probably read the beginning of this chapter and were puzzled. Hmmm, you thought, both your parents are pretty good at looking after you, and both of them want to be involved in the important day-to-day decisions. Both of them want to see you regularly and want you to see the other parent regularly, and both of them want to keep on being a parent. They just don't want to be

married while they do it. Well, relief is on the way. For cooperative families like this we have invented the idea of joint custody.

Joint custody allows both parents to share the decision making
that I talked about at the beginning of this chapter. It can even
allow them to share the time that they have with you.

To start, let's look at joint custody for decision making. If you
live with your mother and see your father only on the weekends or
even weekdays, it is still possible for your mother and father to
share the important decisions about your life. Your parents would
consult with each other as decisions about school, health, religion
and so on have to be made. If an emergency came up, either one of
them could make the decision. I know, it makes sense, doesn't it?
The problem was that a lot of lawyers and parents never thought of
doing this until fairly recently.

Joint custody is a good way of doing things if the parents can
get along. If they argue and end up screaming at each other (or if
just one screams at the other) then it won't work. But if they can
get along, it can sure make life easier.

Some families can even go a step further and share the time
with the children. Many kids find it kind of weird that, when their
parents split up, suddenly they are seeing their father or their
mother only on every second weekend. It seems fake. It is hard to
relax and just be yourself if you have to cram two weeks' worth of
stuff into a weekend. When parents are able to share time with the
kids, this problem disappears. The time can be shared in any way
that suits the family. There are, of course, some limitations because
you don't want to get too confused. Think about the following
though, because these are some situations that families have actually used:

- The children live with the mother one week, from Monday to
  Sunday, then they live with the father the following week, from
  Monday to Sunday.

- The children live with the mother each week, from Sunday
  evening until Thursday evening, then they live with the father
  from Thursday evening until Sunday evening.

- The children live with the mother Monday to Friday each week
  and live with the father Saturday and Sunday each weekend.

- The children live with the father from January 1st to June 30th each year, then they live with the mother from July 1st to December 31st. They work out special arrangements for summer vacation, birthdays and religious holidays.

- The children live with the mother one year, then live with the father the next year.

- The children alternate each month from the mother's place to the father's place.

As you can see, lots of different families use lots of different arrangements. If everyone can cooperate then maybe that kind of arrangement will work for your family. It is not for families where the parents are constantly bickering and arguing. If there is violence, it cannot work. Cooperation and flexibility, those are the keys.

In finishing this section, I would like to give you an example of a good joint custody case that I had a couple of years ago. It involved a very nice family, mom, dad, and two children, Matthew, 13, and Adam, 15. The mom and dad had decided that after 15 years of marriage, they could not continue living together. It was not a separation that was angry or hurtful; to tell you the truth, it seemed more sad than anything else. Neither of the parents had someone new. Neither of them had done something awful to the other. They just could not imagine spending the rest of their lives together.

But, oh! did they agonize over the children. They were literally tearing themselves apart with worry. Neither one of the parents could imagine not seeing the children all the time. There was no way either of them could accept "weekends." They used to say that word to me like it was some horrible disease. What could they do?

One day they decided to speak to the boys about the possibility of separation. The parents were convinced that Matthew and Adam would be crushed. They were wrong. The boys knew that something was wrong and actually had been talking about it for months.

"If it was up to us," Matthew started to say, "...we would only want two things..."

The parents were dumbfounded. "What...what do you want..."

Adam finished Matthew's sentence "...we want you guys to be happy and to make sure that we get to see you equally. We thought that if we all still live in the same neighbourhood and, as long as our bikes are working, we can probably see a lot of you guys..."

The parents looked at each other with their mouths open. "We want to be happy and we certainly want to see you both as much as we can...but... but...we thought..." The mom and dad realized that they had wasted a lot of energy fretting instead of listening. They went to their lawyers with a very specific schedule that they had worked out with the boys. It said that the mom and dad would have "joint physical and legal custody" of Matt and Adam. All decisions would be made together, and they would work out the living arrangements every six months, depending on what was convenient for everyone. The schedule still works without a hitch.

One day, after it was all done, I saw the two boys. I asked if everything had worked out to their satisfaction. Matthew laughed when he looked at Adam, and he said, "They think they have joint custody of us...but we know that we have joint custody of them!" Cool guys.

If your family cannot work out this kind of arrangement, don't worry. The sole custody arrangement I described at the beginning works well for many families too.

I mentioned a little earlier the possible involvement of grandparents, aunts, uncles and cousins in custody and access. Let's look at that in more detail.

GRANDPARENTS, AUNTS, UNCLES, COUSINS...

In all the worry about the separation and divorce it can be easy to forget that a whole bunch of people are thinking about you. Your mom and dad may have brothers and sisters — your aunts and uncles. The aunts and uncles may have kids — your cousins. And it is very possible that you have four grandparents who think and worry about you every day. It is likely that these family members knew about your parents' marriage problems long before you did. Your mom and dad may have discussed the situation with them a long time ago.

In some cases it is hard for relatives to keep out of the arguments that may be going on between your parents. One day your dad may ask his brother for advice and the next day tell him to mind his own business. Your mom's mom may be giving her a lot of advice about what she should be doing — or worse — what she should have done years ago. In short, your other family members may already be involved in the divorce, sometimes to try to help, sometimes not.

I thought we should discuss the role of your larger family for a couple of reasons. First, the positive side: they can be a great source of advice and comfort to you. Most kids have a favourite aunt or uncle whom they trust or a favourite cousin whom they love to share secrets with. If ever there was a good time to call on them for advice and support, it is when your parents are sweating through a divorce. So pick up the phone and call them, if you can, or write them a letter. You may be able to arrange a little visit if it is the right time of year. Tell your mom or dad that you would like to spend some time with the relative. Your parents should understand. The same is true for your grandparents. I have said many times that, in a divorce or separation, grandparents should be like a big pillow that the kids can land on when things blow up.

Now, the negative side. Sometimes relatives choose sides when a separation occurs. Maybe they didn't get along with your mom or dad anyway; maybe they don't like the way that their side of the family is being treated. There may have been some pretty big fights. For whatever reason, some of your aunts, uncles, cousins and grandparents may suddenly be "off limits." Your parents are separating, but you are losing family members and you didn't even do anything. It seems really unfair!

I have seen many situations where the parent with sole custody of the children cuts off contact with the other side of the family. In one case, the mother had remarried and was moving away. The children were very worried that they would never see their grandparents again and the grandparents felt the same way. The family laws of Canada allow grandparents, aunts, uncles and anyone who is involved in a child's life to ask the judge for an access order. In fact, I have met many grandparents who have custody of their grandchildren. The same rules of custody and access apply to them as to parents. This means that if your grandparents, for example, were being prevented from spending time with you, they could ask the judge for an order. The order could provide for specific days and times for them to visit, just like a parent's access.

In every province, family members have been successful in getting court orders to be able to see children after a separation or divorce. Judges have even ordered families to keep up contact with grandparents when there has been no separation. In such cases the parents had simply decided that they were not going to see one side of the family anymore. Although it was expensive and very emotionally draining, the judge ordered that the children be allowed to see their grandparents.

I will never forget one case in which I was involved. The mother and father had been married for about seven years and had one child, a little boy named Jamie. His grandparents — the mom's parents — had spent a lot of time looking after him. They were actually like a day care. Every day the mom would drop Jamie off and the grandparents would look after him until the mom and dad finished work. Jamie loved the arrangement and was very close to his grandparents.

Meanwhile, Jamie's dad had started a business and it wasn't going very well. He tried to borrow money from a bank, but the bank manager thought the dad would not be able to pay back the loan and said, "Sorry." The dad then asked the grandparents to loan him the money and, since they had a little saved up, they said OK. That is when the trouble started.

The business got worse and the dad asked for more money but the grandparents couldn't afford it. Also, they could see that his business was not going to make it. When they said no to a second loan, the dad got angry and took Jamie home early. Then Jamie didn't come the next day or the next. When the grandmother called to find out what was going on, the dad said, "If you don't care about my business, then you don't care about me being able to provide for my family. And if you don't care about that, then you don't care about Jamie! So you can't see him until you loan me more money." Do you believe that? It was blackmail.

The grandparents tried to work things out but the situation got worse and worse. They had to ask a judge to help them. They got an order to see Jamie once a month for one day. Jamie had no idea what was going on until he got older.

There can be many reasons for problems between parents and grandparents, or other family members. I have seen cases where the parents have trouble with drugs, alcohol, gambling, violence, crime and even getting mixed up in cults. The grandparents have come to the rescue in many cases. Sometimes the grandchildren ended up living with the grandparents for years.

Remember that there is always another side to these types of situations — your side. You do not have to see any family member that you do not want to see. Not every aunt, uncle or grandparent is automatically fantastic. Some of them have serious problems too.

In a situation like this, the only advice I can give you is if you are aware of what is happening speak up and be honest with everyone involved. If you want to keep a relationship with a family member, or you want to end one, let the rest of the family know. Remember, if you are old enough to read this book your opinion will count for a lot.

SOME THINGS TO THINK ABOUT: GOOD AND BAD

Let's look at some of the practical problems or things that can come up when your parents separate. These apply whether you are living in a sole custody or joint custody arrangement. First, the problems.

Travelling back and forth between two houses can create problems. Stuff gets lost or it never seems to be in the right place when you need it. You may have to get more organized, yourself, to have what you need in the right house at the right time.

The scheduling of time with your friends or other important events can interfere with the time your parents want to spend with you. I have seen situations where the mom and dad spend all kinds of time, money and energy arguing about when they will see the kids on a particular weekend, only to discover that the kids don't want to go with either parent because they have made their own plans.

Some kids like to talk on the phone to one parent and the other parent doesn't like that. It can be confusing and awkward if you want to talk on the phone about something important but, for whatever reason, you are not able to do it. Long-distance charges just add to this problem.

If you are seeing one of your parents only on the weekends, it can be tough to squeeze in all the stuff he or she may have in mind. The access parent may have been waiting for two weeks to see you and may have planned something really special. But maybe that is one weekend that you are dead tired and just want to crash on the couch. It can feel awkward. It can also feel pretty bad if you are sick and don't feel like going for a visit when it has been arranged.

It can also be tough to visit with all the other family members when you have infrequent visits. Some families expect the kids to keep up with all the aunts, uncles, cousins, grandparents and so on whenever the kids visit with their dad or mom. That can be really hard if you just want to spend some time alone with that parent.

I think one of the most difficult things to sort out can be visits for religious holidays, Thanksgiving, March break, and even summer vacation. These are supposed to be happy times and all you hear is arguing about the visits with family and friends. This happens because parents get a little stressed out around holidays anyway. Some people, for example, get very depressed at Christmas. That can make things tough. It can also be difficult to divide a very small amount of time. There are only 24 hours on December 25th. About ten of them are spent asleep, so that doesn't leave a lot of time to see two whole families, especially if one family lives out of town.

Also, I have talked to kids who say that they feel restless when they move back and forth from one parent's house to the other parent's house. They say that they just start to settle in and it is time to move again.

Another problem is one that your parents may create for you. Message delivery! If your mom and dad are having trouble communicating, they will sometimes ask you to carry messages back and forth. You have probably heard the old line, "Well, you tell your father that if he expects me to...blah blah blah,...then he had better...blah blah blah..." or your father will say, "If your mom thinks I am going to...blah blah blah...then she had better...blah blah blah, so tell her that..." Try to avoid this unpaid job as a courier.

Another awkward part of separation is the travelling. As you may know, there have been angry parents who have actually kidnapped their own children. For example, a father took off to the United States with his children. He told the children that their mother had died and they had to move.

To prevent this from happening, the police at the Canadian border insist that a parent travelling out of the country with a child either have that child's passport or have a letter from the other parent giving permission for the child to be taken out of the country. Recently, I heard of a case where a kid's trip to Florida was cancelled at the border because the parents had not set up the travel papers properly.

Some positive things happen too. For one thing, you will probably have happier parents. Two houses can sometimes be neat. A new room. New stuff for it. Maybe you will have stepbrothers and sisters. And the biggest bonus that sometimes comes with the new arrangement — if your parents can afford it — two vacations, one with each parent.

I have also heard some kids say that their parents paid more attention to them *after* the separation. One kid told me that his parents had turned into a couple of "super parents," each one trying to be the greatest parent ever. I told him to enjoy it while it lasted.

At the end of this chapter I give you some ideas on how to make it a little easier on yourself and your parents when dealing with custody and access.

There are a couple of special problems that we should touch on before we look at ways of dealing with this stuff. Let's look at something called "supervised access."

SUPERVISED ACCESS

In some cases the children are not allowed to visit with a parent or other family member (like a grandfather) unless someone else is there to supervise or watch over the visit. These are known as supervised access visits. They can be agreed to by the people involved or can be ordered by the court. Why would someone need to supervise a visit with a family member? There may be a couple of good reasons. For example, one of your parents may be worried that you will not be safe if you visit alone with the other parent or family member. The person supervising is there to make sure you are safe.

If your parent has a drug or alcohol problem or suffers from a mental illness, then you may need someone there just to watch. We have all heard about the sexual abuse that happens in some families. Or sometimes they worry about kidnapping. If these are a threat to a child's safety, visits need to be supervised. There have been cases where one parent has accused the other parent of being dangerous but nothing has been proved. Until everyone is able to sort out the truth, the visits with that parent need to be supervised.

NAME CHANGE

Another interesting problem may come up — changing your name. What? Change your name? Who is going to do that?

One of the decisions that a parent with sole custody can make is deciding the legal name by which the family and children will be known. If your mother changed her name when she got married to your father, she may decide that she wants to change it back to her maiden name. In many provinces, the court will ask the children what they think and will usually notify the father of the children about the request for the name change. The father may ask the court to stop it. The reason I mention this is not to give you advice on whether to change your name, but to suggest that you speak up about it if you have a preference. You may be signed up for all kinds of activities under one name, and it can be a real drag to have to go around telling everybody that you have a new last name. Oh, by the way, it is only your last name that gets changed. Your first name stays the same unless *you* decide to change that.

SOME SUGGESTIONS

• Try to remember that the divorce is not your fault!

• It is the fault of the adults, and it is their job to fix it — not yours. Be patient and let them work it out.

• Don't forget all the emotional stuff that your parents are going through. They can get angry and depressed. So will you.

• Be as open and as honest as possible with both parents. Once they know what you want, they can plan for what is in your best interest.

• If you are over 9 years of age, you have a right to be heard. Your opinion is important and really can influence the way things are handled.

- Remember, there is more to custody than just where you sleep at night. It also involves making important decisions about your life.

- If you are moving back and forth between two homes, whether for access or because of joint custody, try to make sure everyone is working from the exact same schedule. Make a copy of the calendar each month showing where you should be on each night and weekend. If you see a conflict (your championship baseball game is the same weekend that dad is supposed to take you to the cottage), let your parents know as soon as possible.

- Make a list of the stuff you need for the next day or the Monday after a weekend visit. It can help you avoid forgetting stuff that you will need (like homework).

- Try to stay in contact with the other parent if at all possible. A few little short telephone conversations can make the weekend visit a lot more enjoyable. The same thing applies for other family members. Just because your mom and dad split doesn't mean you should lose contact with all your cousins or aunts and uncles.

- Remember, you cannot please everybody all the time. If conflicts come up, don't panic. Pick the solution that makes the most sense and suits you best.

- Be good to yourself. Relax. If you need to blow off some steam, do it! Speak honestly to somebody that *you* trust.

- Don't get drawn into carrying messages back and forth between your parents. Politely tell them that if they have anything to say to each other they should say it directly. Tell them more than once — parents can be forgetful. If they keep doing it, don't pass on the message. After a couple of missed messages they will get *your* message! Show them this part of the book and tell them I said so!

- Don't get drawn into discussions about money or support. Politely tell your parents that you are not interested. It is for the adults to solve the money problems.

Most important of all, be honest with your parents...and remember...it's not your...well, you know...fault.

7

SUPPORT:
What Will We
Live On?

Money, money, money. So much depends on money, especially in a separation and divorce. Lawyers must be hired, sometimes costing hundreds of dollars an hour. Extra expenses just seem to pile up without much effort. If your mom and dad have separated, they are probably paying for two places to live instead of one. New furniture and appliances and a million other things have to be bought for the second home. Who will pay all the bills?

To make matters worse, although expenses are doubling the amount of money available to the family is not. In many Canadian families both parents work. Your mother may have decided to stay home to look after the children while your father continued to work. Your mother may even have had a really good job or career but decided to spend time with the kids while they were young.

It is very rare for a family to keep the same standard of living after the parents have split up. This can mean getting by with less than you are accustomed to having, at least for a while. Did your family have extra money for a vacation before? Maybe not now.

Did you always get the best pair of running shoes? Maybe not now. Did your family have one home with room for everybody? Maybe not after the separation. In this chapter I thought it might be helpful to look at what happens to the family's financial situation when a separation occurs. This means thinking about the expenses that your whole family will have — for two homes — and the way that those expenses will be paid.

Families either rent their house from someone else or own the house themselves. In either case they usually have to pay a monthly amount for the house they live in. If the house is rented, someone else owns it and the family must pay rent each month to the owner. Rents can vary but can run anywhere from $300 a month to more than $1,000 a month. It depends on where your home is located, how big it is and whether other things are included (like heat, water, cable TV and electricity). If those things are not covered, then your parents must pay them as a separate amount each month. They might pay $70 for electricity, $35 for cable TV and $75 for heating bills. It all adds up to a total of monthly expenses just for the place that you live in. After separation, all of those figures are multiplied by two.

Add to this the cost of food ($400 to $500 a month), the cost of clothes and shoes, school stuff, gifts, bus fares, insurance, a new bike and so on. It adds up to a lot of money each month. Some of the expenses may be things that your mom needs, some may be things for you, and other things may be for other family members. It is all put together in the monthly budget and spread out over a year.

In the next chapter I discuss how family property is divided at separation. We will look at credit cards and how debts can be built up. That is another expense that your parents may have to pay, often a couple of hundred dollars each month on credit cards. It really adds up.

For example, one family that I met during a divorce case found things to be very difficult after the separation. Even before they split up, the mom and dad had some very tight months. There were a few times the family had to cancel things that they were looking forward to. But after the parents separated, the finances got worse. The mom and dad still had the same jobs but now the dad also had to pay rent on an apartment, another gas bill, telephone bill and electric bill — more expenses but the same money coming in.

So who pays? This is where you usually hear the words "support" or "alimony" or "maintenance." They all mean roughly the same thing — after a separation an amount of money is paid by one parent to help the other parent meet expenses until that parent is able to pay his or her own bills. Where the money is paid to help the other parent with his or her own expenses, it is called "spousal support." Where the money is paid to help with child-raising expenses, it is called...you guessed it..."child support," even if the "child" is 15 or 18 or sometimes 20 years old.

SPOUSAL SUPPORT

Let's look at spousal support first. Who gets it? Spouses of course. A spouse is someone considered to be the husband or wife of the other person. This usually means that the people are married, but not always. If a man and woman live together as common-law husband and wife (meaning they never got married, they just started living together) then the couple may be treated as spouses under the law as well. For the details of common-law spouses in Canada, see Chapter 8. The point I want to make here is that when I talk about spousal support it applies to both married people and common-law spouses.

Why would one of your parents get spousal support? This money is supposed to act as a bridge between the way expenses were paid while the husband and wife were together and the way expenses will be paid now that they are going to lead separate lives. In some cases, the fact that the two people were married to each other may have actually caused one of them to be less able to look after him- or herself now that they are separated.

For example, let's say that a man and a woman got married and had two children right away. If the woman was a full-time nurse or a teacher but had quit her job to look after the children, it might be hard for her to go right back to the hospital or the school and start working again. If she was off work for a few years, she might even have to go back to school for a year or two in order to be considered for jobs. In a way, the fact that she got married and had children made it more difficult for her to go back to the work she was trained to do. In a case like this one, the spousal support would be paid to the wife to help her meet her expenses while she went back to school and got retrained. It would continue, perhaps, until she found a good job again.

Who pays the spousal support? It's the person who has a job or who has money to help the other person. In the example I gave above, if the husband had a good job as a computer software designer then he would give a portion of his pay to his wife to help her meet expenses. The money he gives her would be spousal support. It is to help her until she doesn't need his help anymore.

How is it paid? Well, usually it is paid each month by a cheque or bank transfer. It is possible to pay a full year (or more) at once (this is called a lump sum), but most people cannot afford to do that so they pay each month or every two weeks. A couple can agree to any payment schedule that is convenient to them.

How much is paid? It depends on two things: (1) how much the person needs, and (2) how much the person with the job earns. Spousal support could be a few hundred dollars a month or it could be thousands. I once saw a case where the husband paid the wife $4,000 each month after they separated. That added up to $48,000 each year. The husband could afford it because he earned over $150,000 a year. The wife needed the money to pay for her apartment and expenses while she went to school. But I have seen many other cases where the monthly amount for support is a lot less. It is often around $700 a month or less, and for many people that would barely cover rent.

How long does the person pay the support? The spousal support must be paid as long as the person receiving it needs the help. If the settlement ends up in court, the judge will tell the person who is receiving the support that he or she must try to find a job or to get training to be able to find a job. Every person has an obligation to look after themselves financially. Sometimes people need some help to be able to do so, and that is what spousal support is for.

Incidentally, the person receiving the support doesn't have to take just any old job that he or she can get. The person is allowed to look for a job that is well suited to any training or special ability that he or she may have. For example, if, by waiting a few months, the wife might get back into nursing then she should not have to take a job driving a school bus. If the person receiving the spousal support is older, say 60 or 70 years old, and it is unrealistic for him or her to find another job, the support might continue for the rest of his or her life. The same would be true if, for other reasons, it was unrealistic for the person to work. For example, if the person had a physical or mental illness and was unable to hold a job, he or she could receive support indefinitely.

Can spousal support be changed? The amount can be changed and the judge can even order that the spousal support stop if the person no longer needs it. On the other hand, if the person who is paying the support lost his or her job or had a reduction in pay, it is possible for the amount of spousal support to be reduced, even if family needs stayed the same. Any change must be approved by the courts through a variation order.

What if a person doesn't want to pay? This is quite common. If the person who is supposed to pay the spousal support is upset over the way the divorce occurred, or doesn't like the way the property was divided or the custody of the children was decided, he or she may threaten not to pay. I have seen lots of people threaten that they will not pay. Usually they are just saying that because they are angry. Once they calm down and discuss it with their lawyers, they do what the judge has ordered or pay what they promised to pay.

A good reason to pay the support is that the judge can get pretty annoyed if the order is ignored. Across Canada, each province and territory has a system set up to make sure people pay their support orders. Once an order is made by the judge, a copy is sent to the "Enforcement Office." The people who work there are employed by the provincial government. If the order is not paid, they will come after the person with the full force of the law. They can even get the monthly amount deducted right off a person's paycheque (called a garnishment). If they have to, they will have the person's property taken, sold and the money given to the person who is owed the money. In serious cases, if the judge feels that the person could have paid but was holding money back just to be mean, the judge may send the person to jail. This is the toughest penalty the judge can give.

Even though the court order must be obeyed and even though there are Enforcement Offices, many people still refuse to pay and thousands of families struggle along waiting for the money that they need to meet their expenses. In some cases the family must ask the province for help until they get the money. This is called "welfare" or "social assistance."

What if the person cannot pay? This happens too. A person is ordered to pay spousal support but, perhaps, after paying for a while, cannot pay any longer because of illness or unemployment. In that case, the person should go back to the judge right away and ask that the order be changed until he or she gets a new job or business picks up. If the person doesn't get the order changed, then the Enforcement Office will think he or she is just refusing to pay.

One tricky problem is that the cost of going back to court can be expensive. If a person doesn't have the money to pay support then he or she often won't have the money to pay lawyers to go back and change the support order. This is one of the problems in the system that people are trying to fix.

How is one person, or parent, supposed to pay expenses if the amount of support is too low? Very few families can actually live on just the spousal support. Most of them will also receive an amount for child support — we will look at that shortly. It is also common for the person receiving the support to work to help make ends meet. In many cases, a parent might need to work full time *and* get the full child and spousal support to be able to meet the expenses of the family.

CHILD SUPPORT

When the judge is looking at the family situation after the separation and trying to figure out how all these expenses will be met, one of the things that he or she will need to zero in on is the child support. Under Canadian law, each parent has an obligation to support his or her child to the best of his or her ability. In every province and territory it is the same.

Who must pay child support? The parents must both contribute. If, for example, you are in the sole custody of your mother then your father will need to make a monthly payment to your mother to help with the expenses. This can be the case even if your parents have decided on joint custody. Even if you spend a lot of time at your father's place, if he earns more than your mother, he will still need to give her money each month to help meet the expenses at her home. It would be the same if your mother earned more money than your father.

It is usually your biological mother and father who pay and receive child support. But sometimes support can come from someone who, while not your biological father or mother, treated you as if you were his or her child. This might be someone who lived with your mother for a while or your father's second wife. If that person acted like a parent then that person may have to pay child support like a parent.

How is child support paid? Basically, it is paid the same way as spousal support. Usually, each month one parent sends the other parent a cheque to cover the amount that has been ordered by the judge or agreed to by the parents. It is possible to pay the child support in one big lump, but most parents cannot afford to do that.

Some parents have all their payments go through the Enforcement Office. This can change depending upon the province in which you live. Some provinces have set it up so all child support payments go through the Enforcement Office. This makes it easier for the parents and the children who can depend on a regular support payment. Each month the parent waiting for the child support gets a cheque from the Enforcement Office. If the parent who is supposed to pay neglects to send money to the Enforcement Office, then nothing can be passed on to the parent waiting for the money. If the payment is not made, then the same thing will happen as I explained above; the Enforcement Office will enforce the court's order by garnishment or even jail.

Incidentally, support is not provided by one parent saying to the other, "I owe you $350 for child support, but, since I bought Katie new shoes and a knapsack for school, I will deduct $78.56 from the payment." Wrong! The money is paid to the parent in full and then that parent decides how to budget it.

How much is child support? It is like spousal support in that the amount depends on the money that is needed and the ability to pay. If expenses are high and the person earning the money can afford it, then the child support is set at a level to meet the expenses. If the person does not earn much, then the support may be low. It all depends on the family. A formula is used called the Child Support Guidelines. The formula looks at how much the parents earn and then sets a reasonable amount depending on the number of children.

It is possible to have child support orders as low as $75 a month, but I have also seen orders for $3,000 a month. Child support also depends on the number of children and their ages. It costs more to support a 16-year-old who is in high school than it does to support a 2-year-old. All of these things are taken into consideration by the lawyers and the judge when they set the amount for each child.

The judge will also order that the amount of child support increase along with the cost of living. This is called a cost of living allowance (COLA). As inflation increases the cost of day-to-day living, the amount of support also increases. The COLA was designed to avoid having people go back to court every time things got more expensive. It applies to spousal support orders too.

Who gets the money? The parents, of course! A few parents who must pay child support have said "Oh, I think I should give the money to the kids directly...their mother will just waste it on stuff for herself...blah blah blah..." This is not allowed and is a terrible idea (unless the "child" is in university and can manage his or her own budget). Remember that it is the adults who made the problems and it is the adults who should solve them. Dragging kids into the middle by offering to pay money to them directly or even by discussing money stuff with them is a big mistake. I get pretty annoyed when I hear about a father or mother sitting down with the children and stressing them out about money problems. "Your mother shouldn't spend the money on this, she should spend it on that..." or "Your father didn't give me the support cheque until Sunday, and I couldn't deposit it till Monday on my lunch break and that means we can't go to the movies this Saturday...." You don't need to know all that stuff. You can't do anything about it and shouldn't have to worry about it.

I think one of the reasons I get so annoyed is because once I met a little girl, Jill, who was living with her mom. Her dad saw her every second weekend, sometimes more often than that. After a while, Jill began giving her dad a very hard time on visits. Her dad got upset because he thought that maybe she didn't want to see him anymore. He asked her about it and, after some prodding, Jill blew up at him and started yelling about him not paying his child support. Jill said her mom didn't even have enough money to buy food!

The father was stunned. Jill told him that her mom had sat down with her and explained the whole thing — about how her dad was being awful and not paying support. The poor little girl was totally upset about money. It turned out that the reason her dad's support payment had been delayed was because he had changed jobs. His cheque had been held up for two extra weeks. But Jill's mother had dragged her into the middle of all this. Why? Jill couldn't do anything about it. Why make her worry?

If either of your parents start dragging you into that money stuff, I suggest that you just say, "Hold it mom/dad, I am not interested in that stuff. That is for the adults to figure out. Talk to her/him about it." They may need to be reminded a couple of times or just show them this: **Parents, do not bug your kids about money. Don't put them in the middle of your problems. You are the people who got separated. You earn the money. You spend the money. You figure it out. You should do everything in your power to make sure that the money issues are kept as far away from the kids as possible.**

How long is child support paid? The requirement to pay child support can begin even before a child is born. There are expenses when getting ready for a baby and judges will order the father to pay them if the mother needs help.

The obligation to keep paying child support continues until a "child" is no longer a child. That is not much help, is it? A child stops being a child about the age of 16. That does not mean that child support will not be ordered after that age. In some situations child support gets stretched beyond age 16 if the child is still in school. Judges have ordered that parents continue to pay child support until a child has completed his or her first university degree. In one case, a guy tried to get his parents to pay his way through law school. It didn't work; the judge said that he was old enough to start looking after himself. One degree was enough.

As long as a young person is in full-time attendance at school, the support may continue. Also, if a child is disabled or ill it is possible for the child support to continue indefinitely.

But here's a wrinkle — under provincial law a child can change his or her own entitlement to support. It is called "withdrawing from parental control." Great expression, eh? It translates into running away from home or refusing to do what your parents say. If your parents are being reasonable and doing what normal parents do, but you refuse to do as they ask, then a judge is not going to force them to pay your support. In Nova Scotia, a 14-year-old girl was having trouble with her mom. The daughter refused to obey the "house rules" and stayed out all night. Then the girl moved out and went to live with her aunt and uncle, but they had the same problem with her. The girl went back to her mom's place — same problems again. So she left to stay with friends and asked her mom to pay her support. Her mom said, "No way!" and the judge agreed. The girl had withdrawn from parental control, so she stopped getting parental cash.

In B.C., a guy was booted out of school. The judge ruled that it was the same as withdrawing from under the control of his parents. Result — no support.

If, however, your parents treat you badly and are abusive to the point where you cannot take it anymore, then leaving home is not considered an end of their obligation to support you. In other words, if your parents drive you out it is not "withdrawing from parental control."

What if I get a job? In most cases, your getting a job will not affect the amount of child support. The only time that a judge might think it was important is if you were older, and instead of going to school while your support was being paid, you were actually working full time. Otherwise a job is no problem.

What if I move away to go to school and don't live with a parent? This should not matter. The support is still paid to the parent with whom you lived, and they are supposed to pass it on. Some families work it out so that the money is sent directly to the student's bank account from the parent who is paying. That is only for older kids though.

Can my parents agree that there will be no child support? They can try. But the judge can just ignore their agreement and do what he or she thinks is best. I have seen cases where the mother agreed to have custody of the children and said to the father, "As long as you stay away from me and the children I will never ask you for child support." Even if they wrote that agreement out and signed it, it would not be binding. The judge can just throw the agreement out and order support and access.

You can see from all this information that support plays a very big role in keeping both households going after a separation. In many cases it is the key to survival, both for your parents and for you. Just in case you think that you will have to spend the next ten years doing with less, it is my experience that after a couple of years things tend to get back to normal. Other things can happen (either or both of your parents may remarry) and it gradually gets better. Hang in there.

8

SHARING THE FAMILY PROPERTY

If your parents have decided to separate, one of the things they are going to have to figure out is how to share the property they acquired while they were married. They will also need to figure out how to divide all the debts. The bills must still be paid by someone, even though your parents have decided to live separately.

One of the things you will need to accept from the outset is that parents can get pretty stressed out about money and debts and property. There is little you can do to influence decisions when it comes to property division. The reason I am describing all the rules is just so you understand what your parents are going through.

We usually think of the word "property" as meaning things like land (called "real property" by lawyers), a house, a cottage or furniture. But it can include a lot of other things, like money in the bank, pensions, retirement savings (RRSPs), cars, boats, motorcycles, clothes, sports equipment, books, CDs and tapes, TVs, radios and so on. Think about your own home — can you think of something in your home that is not property? Pretty hard, eh?

MARRIED COUPLES

All provinces are a little different in the way their laws try to help families divide property. Some provinces, like Ontario, define property to include businesses or investments and other things not really owned and used by the family. Other provinces include only things actually owned and used by the family itself.

As families acquire these possessions, they may also get something else — debts. A debt is when you borrow money to pay for something and promise to pay the money back, usually with interest. It is very unusual for a family not to have at least some debts. For example, many families will have to borrow money from a bank or trust company to buy a house. This is a special kind of debt known as a mortgage. Some families borrow money to buy a car or a van, others may lease a car. A lease is like renting the car for a long time with a promise to pay the full price of the car over a few years instead of in one shot at the beginning.

Even credit cards are a form of debt because the person with the card uses it on the understanding that he or she will pay back the money spent, or at least part of it, when the bill arrives each month. The credit card company lets the user of the card pay back a little each month — but they charge interest on the amount that you don't pay. So the debt gets a little bigger each month if you don't pay the full amount. It is not unusual for a family to have several credit cards with different amounts owing on each one.

Other kinds of debts that a family can have include loans for renovating or repairing the house. Sometimes your parents might need to fix a leak in the roof or the electrical wiring, so they may borrow from the bank. They may also have borrowed from one of the relatives. It doesn't matter who loaned the money — it must still be paid back and is a debt.

I mention all of this because when your parents split up, they must divide the property *and* the debts. Let's look at an example of property division for a case that I had:

The mom had:

• several pieces of furniture, including an expensive sewing machine;

• a 1995 Honda Prelude;

• lots of personal stuff like skis and scuba-diving equipment;

- savings in the bank of $4,300;
- a pension at work worth $50,000;
- some jewellery;
- a computer, printer and CD-ROM.

The dad had:

- carpentry tools;
- a 1995 Honda Accord;
- lots of personal stuff just like the mom;
- savings in the bank of $26,000;
- no pension at work;
- a computer, printer and fax set-up;
- a large collection of books.

The mom and the dad both had:

- a house worth $204,000;
- most of the furniture in the house, including stereos, TVs, and other stuff like the fridge, stove, washer, dryer and so on;
- a joint bank account with $1,475.

There was lots of other stuff too, but those were the main things that they owned. But, but, but...they owed money too. The mother had one credit card on which she owed $950 and another card on which she owed $2,050. She had purchased the computer on credit. She paid off a little each month. The father had the same problem, he had purchased many of his tools on credit and owed $2,200 on the Honda. He also was trying to pay off a little each month.

They both had to pay back the mortgage on the house. They had borrowed $104,000 when they bought the house and still owed about $98,000. If they sold the house, paid back the mortgage and all their debts, they would have only a little to split between the two of them.

In their case, we decided that it would be better to wait until the market picked up and the school year was over before selling the house. The father got an apartment nearby and the mother stayed in the house. They paid the mortgage each month and slowly paid off the credit-card debts. We tried to make it as painless as possible. Ultimately, only a little money changed hands.

Unfortunately, it is also possible to have more debt than property. That can be difficult because if every creditor wants to be repaid then there is not enough money to do it. It can mean trying to stretch out the money, paying one bill instead of another, and dealing with a lot of family stress.

Sometimes it can also mean that the person who owes the money must take a drastic step — bankruptcy. When a person, or couple, declares bankruptcy, it means that they are admitting that they don't have enough money to pay all their debts. The people who are owed the money can get pretty upset because they may need that money to pay their own debts. In a bankruptcy, creditors will usually take all the property belonging to the person who owes the money and sell it to pay off the debts. Then a court will usually make an order wiping out the remaining debt. This last part is not as great as it sounds because, once a person has gone bankrupt, it can be very hard to borrow money again. It can be embarrassing when a store refuses to give one of your parents a credit card because he or she went bankrupt. It often takes five years or more after the bankruptcy before a person can borrow money for any purpose.

Don't worry that your parents may go bankrupt just because they are separating. It doesn't happen to every family. Bankruptcy is more likely to be caused by a business failing or some other big financial problem than by a divorce.

When your parents separate they must figure out all of this stuff, so you can see why they may be under a lot of pressure and worried. When they go in to meet with their lawyers — and, remember, each parent will have his or her own lawyer — they will be asked to fill out some forms that summarize all the property and debts that they may have. (See the Appendices for a sample of this form.) This information will help the lawyers to make suggestions on how to divide the property and debts. The lawyer may say to your mom, "Well, Jessica, if this went to court and the judge saw this financial information, I think he or she would divide it like this..." Then the lawyer would give his or her opinion based on the law of that province or territory.

Across town, your dad's lawyer may be giving him a similar opinion. The two lawyers will then try to negotiate a settlement of the property and the debts. If your parents cannot agree, they may use a mediator (see Chapter 9) to help them reach an agreement. If they still cannot agree, then they may have to go to court and let a judge decide for them.

If your parents go to court, the judge will try to follow a formula provided by the law of their province. The formulas are a little different for each province and territory, but the goals are roughly the same. The court wants to include as much property as possible in the division (taking account of debts at the same time), give each piece of property a fair value and then divide the total fairly between your parents.

The judge tries to make sure that, after all the debts have been paid, each parent — and you — has something to live on as you all start over. A good way to think of this property sharing is to think of the marriage as a special kind of business. Your mom and dad were the partners in the business. Now that they are ending the business they should share the property, profits and losses between them. That's fair.

Of course, there are always exceptions to the rules. One exception concerns the kind of property that is shared. I mentioned earlier all the different things that are considered property and we saw that just about everything is included. When the laws were made, however, our legislators (lawmakers) thought that some things, even though they were property, should still not be shared. For example, if your mom was in a car accident five years before the separation and sued the guy that smashed into her, and if the judge in that case awarded her $100,000 for all her pain and suffering, then that money would not be shared in a divorce. Another example is if your grandfather died and left your dad $100,000 in his will. It might be unfair to split that up in a divorce.

If your mom and dad signed a marriage contract (see Chapter 12) and in it they agreed that your mom's share of a business she had with her sister would not be shared in the case of a divorce, then that contract would be respected. Parents, therefore, sometimes agree not to divide things if they get divorced.

There are also some special rules about the home that you and your parents live in. The court tries to make sure that this piece of property, which is usually the biggest thing the family has, is divided fairly between your parents, no matter what. So, if your mom spent the money from the car accident on a new roof for the house, she might lose the right to keep that money separate in a divorce. The same might be true for your father's inheritance. In most provinces, no matter who put the money into the house, the court tries to divide its value fairly.

It can be tough facing the fact that the family home must be sold. It is very common in divorces that people decide that they will sell the house, pay off the mortgage and divide whatever is left over. I think kids find this really upsetting because it seems like everything is being turned upside down all at once. Unfortunately, people often just don't have a choice. If the debts are to be paid, then the house must be sold. The only time the court will let one of the people in the marriage keep the whole house is if both people agreed in a marriage contract that it would not be shared.

The same thing may be true of who gets to stay in the house when your mom and dad separate. The court does not always care who owns the house or how it will be divided. The judge may order that one of your parents can live in the house and that the other parent must move out, at least until the whole thing is settled. The judge may do this if, for example, your mom will have custody of the children and, therefore, must live near your school until the end of the year. This is sometimes called "exclusive possession" of the home. It means one parent stays in the home, usually with the kids. It also may be used if one of your parents has been violent with the other and is ordered to stay away.

What does all this mean to you? What about your stuff? If your parents are separating, it means that there will be two homes instead of one. Your mom may stay in the house that you have been living in and your dad may rent an apartment nearby or your mom may move in with her mother and father. If you will be spending time at both places then you may wonder where your stuff will go.

One thing that you should not worry about is your mom and dad dividing your stuff or selling it. When families separate, the children's property is usually left alone. You keep what is yours. That does not solve the problem of where to keep it if there are now two houses. You cannot be expected to drag it back and forth every time you see one of your parents. Most kids keep their stuff at the home of the parent who has custody. If they usually use a particular item when they are at their other parent's house, then they may just leave it there. For example, if your dad always takes you to baseball practice or figure skating, you may just want to leave that stuff at his house. That could make it hard to practice, though, so some kids do carry their equipment back and forth. Each family needs to do what is right for them and then stick to the plan. Don't ever be afraid to speak up for what would be best for you.

It is not always realistic to think that you can have two of everything — one for each house — two bikes, two baseball gloves, two pairs of skates, two sets of clothes and so on. Often it is just too expensive for the family. I have also mentioned a couple of times that you will probably need to make do with less. Most families cannot keep the same lifestyle after they split up. Two homes cost more than one. So you may notice a change in the kinds of things that your parents buy. There will be less money to go around. But don't worry about that stuff. As long as there is food, a roof over your head and the other normal stuff, you'll get by.

Please don't do what one kid — David — did. He saw that his mom had less money after the separation, so he decided that he would eat less to save money. He was being a really nice kid for trying to help his mom, but he was going about it the wrong way. By eating less he was saving about $3 a month at most. But he was not helping his health. His mom noticed that he was not asking for the usual extra load of chicken nuggets. He tried to cover up but finally confessed to his mom, "I'm trying to save you money on the food bills." She told me later that she almost started to cry, but she just gave him a big hug instead. She said, "I appreciate you trying to help out but don't worry about that stuff. Eat, be happy and let me figure out the menu!" His appetite came back pretty fast.

Now that we know about the ups and downs of dividing the property and the debts of people who are married, let's look at how the legal system works in the case of parents who are living in a common-law relationship (not married).

COMMON-LAW RELATIONSHIPS

I mentioned in Chapter 1 that the information in this book applies whether your mother and father are married or living together. When we think of a so-called "normal" family, we tend to think of a family that has a woman and man who got married, started to live together and then had their kids. There are now many variations on the idea of what's "normal." Canadian families are started, changed, moved around and blended together in many, many different ways. In this section, I want to give you basic information on what is known as "living common law."

In a nutshell, a common-law relationship is the same as a marriage. The only thing that is missing is the actual marriage. The couple live together, they share everything, they sleep together, they sometimes have children, and, basically, they do everything that married people do — except actually get married. This is quite legal and millions of Canadians form such relationships every year.

Why would two people, who act like a husband and wife, not get married? Well, there may be good reasons for them not to get married. Maybe they just don't want to be married. Maybe they think that it is an unnecessary formality. I have met couples who say that they love each other and will stay together forever without needing to make a lot of legal promises. I have two very good friends who have lived together for 15 years, own two houses together, have a business and have two little girls. They still think it is more romantic to live together without a marriage certificate.

Some people do not get married because they *cannot* get married. If they are already married to someone else, but separated from them and maybe waiting to be divorced, then they cannot legally marry anyone else. Lawyers frequently meet clients who must live common law with a new person while they wait for their divorce.

In Canada, it is a crime to get married to someone if you are already married. It is called "bigamy." I once had a case where a man and a woman separated after being married for about seven years. They went to their lawyers and asked for a divorce. It takes several months for the divorce paperwork to go through the courts, even if everybody agrees to it being done. One day, out of the blue, a woman telephoned me and asked if I was one of the lawyers involved in the divorce. I said yes. She asked if she could have a copy of the divorce papers. I asked her who she was and why she was so interested in the divorce. She said, "I married the man in Florida about two weeks ago!" I said that was impossible because he was not yet divorced in Ontario. She said, "Oh, I guess that is why he was charged with bigamy last week." I checked and he was actually charged with a criminal offence. He lied when the justice of the peace had asked if he had ever been married before.

But going back to where I left off, some people live together without getting married because they want to see if it will work out. Living together is like an experiment. If it works, then they may get married. If they do not like living with that person, then they can just move out. No divorce is needed because they were never married.

There are some people who do not get married because they were married before. It didn't work out so they are a little afraid to try it again.

You may be wondering whether a person becomes "common law" the minute he or she moves in with somebody. At what point is a couple considered to be "living common law" and with legal obligations? Well, it depends on several things. First, the law that applies to common-law couples is different from province to province. Some provinces, like Alberta, do not even recognize the concept of common-law couples. People in Alberta still live together without getting married, but if they split up they do not have any legal protection.

In other provinces and territories common-law spouses are recognized depending on the amount of time that the couple must live together. The time varies from province to province. The following is a list of the various provincial and territorial rules:

• British Columbia — two years of living together,

• Saskatchewan — three years or a child is born while the couple is living together,

• Manitoba — five years together or one year and a child is born while the couple is living together,

• Ontario — three years or a child is born while the couple is living together,

• New Brunswick — three years of living together,

- Nova Scotia — one year of living together,
- Newfoundland — one year and a child is born while the couple is living together,
- Yukon — the couple has a relationship of some permanence,
- Alberta, Quebec, Prince Edward Island and the Northwest Territories do not formally recognize common-law couples.

You may have noticed from the list that some provinces will recognize a couple as common-law spouses if they live together and have a child. Usually the relationship between the couple must be fairly serious. A couple does not automatically become common-law just because a baby is born. That is what is meant by a relationship of "some permanence."

The next important questions about common-law couples are: What does that mean? If your parents live common law, what rights do they have? What obligations do they have? As long as a couple live together and are happy no one will care, but the problems come when people who are living common law buy property together, have children, make plans together and *then* they separate! They don't need a divorce but....What will happen to the kids? The house they bought together? How will they live once they separate? These are the same kinds of problems married people face, but the way the problems are solved is not exactly the same.

It does not matter that a couple is living common law when it comes to making decisions about kids. All of the things we learned about custody, access and child support still apply. So, if your mother and father are not married to each other but are separating, the same rules for those areas apply. It's just as if they were married and about to get a divorce.

Things can get a little tricky, however, when a common-law couple separates and must divide their property. You remember from Chapter 4 that, when the couple is married, there are laws in each province and territory that tell them how to divide their property when they separate. A married couple can always agree to divide it any way they want, but if they cannot agree then the property division law can be used. The basic rule is to try to divide equally everything that they collected between the day they got married and the day they separated. That's fair enough.

If the couple did not get married and was living common law, those laws do not apply. They may be able to agree on how to divide the property, and that is fine, but if they cannot agree then the judge may have to step in. Since there are no laws to guide common law property division, the judge looks at each case individually. The general approach that the judge would use for your mother and father would be something like this:

- If one person owned the property when the couple started to live together, then that person keeps it.

- If the couple bought the property together, then one person should keep it and pay the other person the amount that the other contributed.

- If the couple cannot agree on who should keep the property, then sell it and split the money.

- If one person gave the other person the property as a gift, then he or she should keep the gift.

- If the couple bought something (like a house) together, but the papers only refer to one name, then that person may hold the house "in trust" for them both to share. Holding something in trust means protecting it for both people, even though both names are not on the deed.

The judge will try to divide things fairly based on what each person contributed to the purchase of particular pieces of property. This is different from the way the judge does it for married people. Do you see the difference? If you're married, the judge divides everything equally. It does not matter who bought or paid for things. But if a couple lives common law, then they will usually get out only what they put in.

Sometimes the court may adjust the common-law couple's property division if one of them put in something other than money. For example, if the woman in the relationship had stayed home from her regular job for a year in order to renovate the house that was owned by the man, then she should get something out of it if they separate. The man would have had to pay someone to do the work, so he saved money by the woman doing the renovation. The same might be true if the woman had spent all of her time looking after the children. The judge might want to adjust the amount of property she would get if she had done all, or most, of the child care.

Basically, there is very little protection for common-law couples if their relationship goes sour and they decide to separate and divide their property. In a later chapter I will explain one of the ways that this problem can be avoided — it is called a "cohabitation agreement." It is a "marriage contract" for people who are not married. If your parents find new partners after their divorce, as they often do, it would be smart for them to have a cohabitation agreement.

One area where there is some special protection for common-law couples (assuming they meet the provincial rules where they live) is in the area of spousal support. When a common-law couple separates, the court will look at the possible need for some financial help from one spouse for the other. If one needs the help and the other can afford to pay, then the court will order that the help be given indefinitely or for a fixed time. So, in this respect, the couple is treated the same as if they were married.

This information about legally married and common-law spouses was intended to give you a big overview of how the property and debts are divided at the time of separation. Now let's look at the way that lawyers and families work together to settle cases or, if they cannot settle, the way the cases end up in court.

9 SETTLING, GOING TO COURT AND SOME NEW WAYS TO SOLVE PROBLEMS

When kids think of lawyers, they usually think of someone arguing in a courtroom, perhaps cross-examining a witness. That is the
way lawyers are shown on television and for a pretty good reason
— it is exciting to be in a courtroom. There can be lots of drama
and tension. Everyone must concentrate on the evidence and the
witnesses. It can be very draining by the end of the day because
the emotions are exhausting. But, do you know what? In all the
years that I have been in court with clients and in all the cases that
I have been involved in, I have never had a client say to me, "Wow,
that was the most exciting thing I have ever done! I really enjoyed
being in court." No one has ever said that to me. The reason why
is this — it is only the lawyers who like court! We find it exciting;
we like the drama. The clients hate it! Clients have told me that
going to court was one of the worst experiences of their lives.
Even when they won.

So you're probably wondering, "If so many people hate going
to court, why are the lawyers and courts so busy?" Good question.
When your parents decide to divorce, they are either going to
come to an agreement (called settling the case) or going to disagree and end up in front of a judge (called not settling a case).
Let's take a look at these choices.

SETTLING A CASE

After the people involved have consulted with their lawyers and have had a chance to think about the advice they have been given, the lawyers will begin to negotiate. The negotiations may take place on the telephone or may be carried on by letters that are written back and forth. The legal system always tries to encourage these kinds of negotiations. One of the ways to negotiate is through "without prejudice" discussions. You have probably heard that expression on television when lawyers are talking to each other. They may say something like, "I like your suggestion for a settlement, Jessica. I would like to discuss it with my client without prejudice to his right to sue your client for a million dollars." What they mean is that they don't want the other lawyer to turn around and use the information against them at a later date.

For example, in one case a father and mother were arguing about custody of their son, Andrew. Both of them said that they wanted sole custody, but the father was thinking about changing his approach to the issue of custody. He wanted to suggest to the mother that maybe she should have sole custody, but only if he could see Andrew two nights a week and on weekends. He didn't want the mother's lawyer to say, "Ah ha! You really don't want custody because in this letter you say that his mother should have custody! Wait till I show the judge this letter..." If every suggestion the father made could end up in court, then how could he ever talk about settling?

To prevent this from happening, lawyers and judges have agreed that if a client sends a letter discussing settling but doesn't want the other side to use the letter in court, the lawyer should write the words "without prejudice" across the top of the letter. In the case of Andrew that is what his father's lawyer did. He wrote a letter to the mother's lawyer. It said "without prejudice" at the top and in it he suggested the custody/access arrangement. The mother loved the idea, and the case was settled. But if the lawyer had not sent that letter, it might have gone all the way to an expensive court hearing.

It is very common to hear lawyers use the expression "without prejudice" when discussing cases on the telephone or when writing to each other. If any lawyer tries to use "without prejudice" information or tells the judge something that was supposed to stay just between the lawyers and clients, he or she can get into trouble with the judge. The reason for this is important so everyone works very hard to protect it.

As the letters and discussions continue, your parents and their lawyers may adjust their positions a little. They may be able to resolve the division of family property and the debts. If they agree, then one lawyer will write a letter to the lawyer on the other side to confirm that part of the settlement. Then both sides keep negotiating. If they find that they have settled all the issues, they will do one of three things: (1) ask the judge for a "judgment on consent," (2) write up "Minutes of Settlement," or (3) write up a separation agreement. Let's look at each one briefly.

Judgment On Consent

This is where the people involved in the family law case have decided how they think the matter can be settled. If the lawyers have already started the paperwork at the courthouse, it is possible to get the judge to make an order to which everyone agrees. The lawyers will prepare a summary of the settlement and take it to the judge. He or she will look it over and, if it appears that everyone agrees, then the judge will make the judgment. This is a good way to wrap up all the details. Later, if one of your parents changes his or her mind, the other parent has a court judgment that can be enforced.

Minutes Of Settlement

This is the document that lawyers use to summarize the settlement of a case. Imagine that everyone has been arguing for weeks, unable to settle the important issues. As they wait in the hallway at the court office, your mother and father suddenly start talking and figure out a way to settle the case. The lawyers are thrilled but do not want to take the chance that if they wait until the next day to write up the settlement, one of your parents might change his or her mind. When this happens a lawyer may use his briefcase as a makeshift desk and write out by hand the details of the settlement. The lawyer will write a heading "Minutes of Settlement," just like the minutes of a meeting. The people sign at the bottom, the lawyers witness the signatures and the settlement is done. Some lawyers will go an extra step and ask the judge to read the minutes of settlement and make a consent judgment.

Separation Agreements

The most popular method for settling a family law case is a separation agreement. This is a contract that is signed by the husband and wife and in it they agree to do certain things. It can be very detailed and is used by people who were married or who were living common law.

To be official and legal, the agreement must be written, signed by both people and witnessed. Most law offices have computers with hundreds of different paragraphs stored in the memory. The lawyer goes through the computer and picks out the paragraphs that are best suited to the needs of the people involved. Once the agreement is signed it is like any contract — binding and enforceable. It can deal with custody, access, property division, debts, the house, support and anything else.

There are many advantages to signing a separation agreement. It is less expensive than going to court. It can be very detailed and can make arrangements for as much stuff as the people need to cover. It can be enforced by the court if someone tries to back out later. It also makes a lot of sense for people to make a settlement that is perfect for them rather than letting a judge decide.

I put some sample paragraphs in the back of this book so you could see what a real separation agreement looks like. One of the things I remind parents about is this — while they should be the ones who decide what the settlement should be, they should not be the ones to draft their own agreement. It is *always* a very good idea to get a lawyer to look at the agreement. There might well be some new way of solving a problem or a better way of drafting the words, so your parents should always get independent legal advice before signing.

It is possible in some very special situations to get a judge to throw out a separation agreement. If one person was tricked into signing or was fooled into thinking that the agreement was actually something else, then a judge may tear it up and make the couple start all over. That does not happen very often, but in really bad cases of trickery or lying it can. Lawyers guard against that happening.

So you can see there are lots of ways to settle the case if the people are reasonable and work together. But what if your parents don't settle or what if one of them is totally unreasonable? Then they end up in court!

UH! OH! NOT SETTLING THE CASE

Most divorce cases settle without ever having to go to court. One study concluded that almost 90 percent of the cases will settle without having to go to court, except to finalize the papers. But that still leaves a lot of people who, for some reason, cannot agree. It may be that they are both unreasonable or they both think that they are absolutely correct. On the other hand, it may be just one person preventing a settlement. It takes two people to resolve a case but only one to block it. No matter what the cause, if a couple can't settle, they will eventually need to appear in front of a judge.

Just getting an appointment with the judge is a problem. Judges are very busy, so weeks and months can go by before time is available. Delays and postponements (called adjournments) are common.

Lawyers get a laugh out of trials on television. The people meet the lawyer for the first time at the beginning of the show. Half an hour later they are in court in the middle of an exciting trial. Real life is very different. Cases can drag on for months or years. Negotiations can be slow and very boring. The rules of court are complicated and lots of paperwork has to be done. Lawyers will spend dozens of hours preparing all this stuff. Remember that they are charging $200 or $300 an hour, so a divorce can cost your parents thousands of dollars.

Your parents must take all of this into consideration when deciding whether to settle the case. The lawyers will keep reminding your parents that there is no point spending $10,000 on a trial if they are arguing over $5,000. The cost of going to trial sometimes forces people to settle even though they really don't want to.

THE COURTROOM

I have included below a diagram of a typical Canadian courtroom. At one end of the room is the bench where the judge sits. In front of the judge's bench is a long table for the court clerks to do their work, such as keeping track of documents. The court reporter sits near the clerics table so that he or she can hear everything that is said. Just to the side of the judge there is a box where the witnesses stand when giving evidence. A little further back are two long tables for the lawyers for the two sides to spread out their work. Your parents will sit beside their lawyers at this table. The lawyers may have a clerk assist them or, perhaps, a junior lawyer may help.

At the back of the courtroom is a seating area for the public. Sometimes the courtroom can be crowded; sometimes the judge keeps the hearing as private as possible. You will never see a jury in a family law case or a divorce — never. It is always a judge.

During the trial the judge will listen to the evidence. The person who started the divorce (if that is what is being requested) is called the petitioner; the other person is called the respondent. The petitioner, say your mom, goes first and her lawyer calls a witness. Her lawyer asks the witness some questions and then sits down. The witness is then cross-examined by your dad's lawyer.

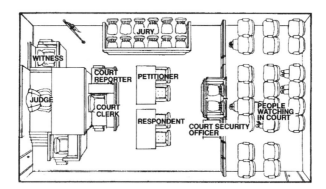

This procedure is followed for each witness until the petitioner, your mom, has called all of her witnesses. Then the respondent, your dad, and his lawyer do the same thing with his witnesses. At the end the two lawyers summarize the evidence for the judge and suggest how they think the case should be decided. The judge may decide right away or may want to think about it for a while. When the judge decides to think about the issues, that is called "reserving judgment." The court clerk calls the lawyers once the decision is ready.

If one or both of the people disagree with the judge's decision, it is possible to appeal the decision to a higher court. This is rarely done in divorce cases simply because it is so expensive.

All of this can take a couple of years and can cost thousands of dollars. At the end of the case, when one of the people has "lost" and the other has "won" (by win I mean that the judge agrees with that person's suggestion for how to resolve the case), the judge will ask a very important question, "What do you want to do about costs?" This actually means, how much should the person who lost pay to the person who won in order to cover their legal costs? That's right, the person who lost must pay! That is one of the reasons people go to lawyers — to make sure that they are going to trial with at least a reasonable shot at having the judge agree with them.

The judge will set the amount of costs that must be paid. The bad news is that this never covers the whole cost of the lawyer's bills. It usually covers about 50 to 60 percent. The rest must be paid by the person who won. (That person may not feel much like a winner when he or she gets the bill.)

Because going to court is so expensive, and because a decision by a judge never seems as fair as one that is worked out by cooperative people, everyone tries to avoid having a divorce end up in court. One procedure is often used by lawyers to put on pressure when one person is being unreasonable. Remember I said that one person can block a settlement? There is a way to deal with that. It's called an "Offer to Settle." It sort of fits in between the first part of this chapter, "Settling," and this part, "Not Settling."

When the lawyers have a good idea of what the case is all about and feel confident about how a judge will decide it, they sometimes send each other written "Offers to Settle." These are "without prejudice" proposals to settle the case. In a way, the lawyer is saying "I think the judge will decide the case as follows..." The offer is typed out and very clear. The reason these offers put pressure on the other side is that the lawyers will show them to the judge after he or she has given the judgment. Until then the offers

are kept confidential. Once the judge has given the decision, however, the lawyers will pull out their offers to settle and say to the
judge, "Your Honour, I offered to settle the case exactly the same
way six months ago. We had this trial for nothing!" The judge will
read it over and, if it is true, the person who rejected the offer will
pay all the costs of the winner. Ouch!

So you can see, the difference between settling and not settling
can be time, money and, perhaps, a person's sanity! Let's look at
one of the things that has been invented to help people settle —
mediation.

AN ALTERNATIVE TO COURT — MEDIATION

After hearing about all of the twists and turns and expense of the
court system, you may wonder why anyone would ever use that
method to solve a family's problems. Fair enough, I wonder about
it myself. It seems like an extra punishment to go through, as if a
divorce weren't tough enough already. The problems of going to
court don't ever seem to discourage people from doing it, though.
The bottom line is that people will separate and divorce no matter
what. The interesting questions remain: Is there an easier way to
do this? Is there a system that treats families with a little more sen-
sitivity? The answer to both questions is "Yes." It is called mediation and has actually been around for years.

Mediation is a way for the family to sit down with a neutral
third person to try to figure out a way of settling all the problems.
Your school may use mediators in the schoolyard to help kids settle their fights or arguments. If the mediator cannot solve the
problem, then he or she calls a teacher. It is the same with divorce
and other family law cases. If the mediator cannot solve the problem, then it's back to a judge.

The mediator does not decide how the problems will be
solved. He or she listens to your parents, asks them questions
and makes suggestions. But it is the parents who must make the
decisions and — importantly — they must agree. That is the
point of mediation: your parents are supposed to find a way to
agree. If they agree on what is supposed to happen, say, on how
they will be able to spend time with you, then everything can go
a lot smoother. Mediation can also be less expensive. But the

best thing about your parents' agreeing to something is that, if they agree, then they are more likely to do it.

In many cases, when a judge has ordered a parent to do something that he or she really doesn't want to do, that parent may not obey the court order right away. This just makes things more difficult. Eventually, the parent will have to obey the judge because that is the law. Disobeying a court order is called contempt of court and can lead to fines or even jail terms.

Both parents have to agree on who will be the mediator. There are lots of people, both men and women, who do this type of work. They have been specially trained to help couples agree on solutions to problems. I took a course on how to be a mediator and found it very interesting. The first step for the mediator is to get the parents to listen to each other. That can be tough if they are angry, or if they think they have heard everything there is to hear. The mediator's next step is to change the language or words that the parents use to describe what they want. It is common to hear a parent say, "I must have custody of the kids..." or "I must have the car..." or "I want $1,000 each month to cover expenses..." and so on. Did you notice the words "want" and "must"? Remember all those times your mom and dad or teacher said, "There is a big difference between what you *want* and what you *need*..."? Unfortunately, most parents forget that advice the minute they start having problems. Or they assume that what *they* want is what the *children* want.

The mediator must do two things: first, remind your parents to talk about what they need, not what they want; second, remind your parents to talk about what *you* need. The mediator will ask your parents, "What do the children think? How are they dealing with this? What do they say they want? What do they need?" The mediator may even want to meet with you to talk about what you want.

The way that the mediator changes the language can take time but, eventually, your parents will start talking about needs, not wants. As the discussion gets going, parents can become very creative and, sometimes, solve everything at once. When I say "solve" I do not mean solve the problem of why they are splitting up. If parents are meeting with a mediator it is to make the separation easier on everyone, not to help them get back together.

If your parents are using a mediator it does not mean that there are no lawyers involved. They will still need lawyers to write up any agreement and make sure it is a fair deal for both sides. The lawyers will also make sure the agreement is signed and all the paperwork is done.

I thought that you might find this information useful because not all parents know about mediation. You may want to suggest it to them if they are having trouble getting things settled or are threatening to go to court. The other reason I mentioned it is because the mediator will be asking questions about your needs and your wants. If you are able to tell your parents what you need and what you want, you will be able to help find a solution. This means thinking about some of the choices that you have, and it means being honest.

Nobody wants to hurt somebody else's feelings. Kids, especially, do not want to hurt their parents' feelings, so sometimes they will tell a parent what they think that parent wants to hear. But that kind of double talk will just confuse everybody. Use the worksheets at the end of the book to figure out what you need and want. It will help you and your mom and dad.

10 VIOLENCE IN YOUR HOME?

Several years ago I was working in my office when a new client, an older woman, arrived for some advice about a separation and a divorce. When I walked into the reception area, I saw her sitting there with three of her daughters. The mother had obviously been beaten up and looked very sad. With the help of her daughters, she got into my office where she explained that her husband of 25 years had beaten her up and thrown her out of the family home. The husband was still back at the house drinking.

I was in shock. As a young lawyer I had never seen anything like this. I had heard about violence but I had never thought about someone beating up a nice, older woman with beautiful kids.

My initial shock got worse as the woman told her story. I was not the first lawyer that the woman had consulted. The previous week, she had gone to the lawyer who had handled the purchase of her home. He was not a family law lawyer and was very busy with real estate work. After talking to her for a while, he suggested that she go home and try to work things out. Court was expensive and slow. Did she really want to separate? Her husband had done crazy things before and it had all blown over. Why overreact now?

The woman didn't know what to do and was ready to go back home when one of her daughters stopped her. She insisted that her mom see a lawyer who was experienced in family law. The mother decided to give it one more try and so she had come to see me.

I put aside everything else on my desk and spent the rest of the day and that night working on her case. She told me that her husband had been abusive for years. She had stayed because of the children, because she was afraid of what he might do and because she thought she could not get a job. The children were aware of what had been going on and couldn't understand why their mom, this great woman that they loved, would not leave. They loved their dad too, but could no longer accept a situation that was obviously wrong.

Within the next 24 hours, we got a judge's order for custody of the younger children, support and possession of the home. More importantly, we got a restraining order prohibiting the husband from contacting the family. It was a very satisfying result. At the end of it, though, I thought that it was really the daughter who had saved her mom. Thanks to her, her mom didn't go back to the violence in that house. The girl may have saved her mom's life.

In this chapter I would like to take a look at the ugly secret that exists in many Canadian homes — the secret of domestic violence.

What is "domestic violence"? Other terms are sometimes used — "wife assault" or "wife battering" or "wife abuse." When we talk about this subject we are talking about acts of violence in the family, most often done by men against their wives, common-law partners, girlfriends or children. One legal definition is as follows:

> ... the intent by the husband to intimidate either by threat or by the use of physical force on the wife's person or property. The purpose of the assault is to control her behaviour by the inducement of fear ...

(Translation: Threatening to hurt someone to get them to do what you want.)

It is amazing what some people will do to someone they say they love: slapping, punching, kicking, choking, even pinching. There have been cases of women being burned, beaten with belts, stabbed and even shot. Women have even been killed by abusive husbands. Assaults can include sexual attacks, humiliation or being forced to watch pornography.

Sometimes the abuse is psychological — threats, insults, belittling and embarrassment. I have seen cases where women's clothes were ripped up, photos were burned, pets were threatened or injured and money taken. Some women are never actually hit but think they will be hit unless they do what they're told. There is a similar pattern to the treatment these women receive whether the abuse is physical or psychological. *This treatment can include young girls as well, so, girls, pay attention.*

The men who commit abuse have a lot in common too. For some reason, abusive men can be quite charming (I guess they would have to be, with all the grief they inflict). These men really come on strong and try to be romantic. They can be a little moody but fun when they want to be. Then the violence starts. A little bit of tension builds up until it explodes in yelling and maybe even hitting. Here is the amazing part — surprise — it's the woman's fault. The woman caused it to happen because of something she said or did. But next thing you know, the man is apologizing like crazy and is back to his old charming self. It will never happen again...he says.

Oh, but it will happen again...and again and again. Same pattern, always the woman's fault and then the abject apology and the charm. Eventually, the woman or girl is worn down and actually starts to believe that it somehow *is* her fault. She is hooked, possibly for life. She may not get out of this situation until she is 50 years old, covered in bruises, sitting in the lawyer's office with her kids...or she may never get out. Unless, of course, she keeps reading....

A puzzling thing about violence in the home is the difficulty that the victim faces in trying to overcome the "wearing down." It can be very hard for a woman to leave even though the situation is awful, even dangerous.

Let's get one thing straight before we go any further — it is not your responsibility to save your parents if they are in this situation. Be supportive, but be careful, you can't stop the violence all by yourself. In the story I told you at the beginning of this chapter, the daughters did not stop the violence. Instead, they got their mom in touch with someone who could help her. Later, they did the same thing for their dad — they got him to go for counselling for his alcoholism.

There was something else in that case that was unusual — the mom listened to the advice of the daughter and got a second opinion right away. Many young people in violent homes have told me that they've begged their moms to leave a thousand times, but the moms just couldn't bring themselves to get out. Something held them there.

One young guy told me that he was getting awfully angry with his mom because she wouldn't do anything to help herself. He said he was losing respect for her, that he almost hit her himself one day because he was totally frustrated. It was then that he knew that he was "contaminated" by his father's violence.

The reason I mention this is because you will need patience too. It is not easy for someone to break out of the cycle. One study of domestic violence concluded that a woman may be assaulted, on average, 35 times before she tries to leave the home. That's three times a month for a year! This kind of repeated violence happens a lot. All of the studies that have been done reveal that domestic violence goes on in many homes across Canada. It doesn't matter whether you are rich, poor, famous, what your religion is, or your ethnic or racial background. Violence can happen in anyone's home.

I bet there is a guy reading this right now, saying to himself, "Hey, this isn't fair! Sometimes men are hit by their wives or girlfriends too." That's true. Physical violence by women against men does happen. But it does not happen nearly as much. Any man who is being assaulted by his wife or girlfriend should get help too. I am not saying that we should ignore *that* problem. I am saying that the really big problem is men being violent with women and kids. Let's tackle that problem. If you are a guy reading this, you can help. Keep reading.

What about those kids who live with and see this stuff in their homes? They learn a lesson from it. The boys learn that being violent is how they are supposed to treat their girlfriends or their wives. Take that guy I mentioned a minute ago — he was going to hit his mother! He learned that somewhere.

The girls in violent homes learn that they have no real worth in society. The hidden lesson for them is that it is normal for women to be beaten and threatened by their boyfriends or husbands or even their sons.

Kids in these homes who see this stuff day after day suffer from depression, fear, anger and confusion. Nobody wants or should have a life like that.

THE MYTHS

Let's get rid of some myths at the outset. The experts say that there are nine misconceptions, or myths, about domestic violence. Think about these:

Myth 1. Domestic violence is caused by mental illness.
Not true. These people are quite sane; they just cannot control their anger.

Myth 2. Domestic violence is caused by alcohol.
Not true. Many assaults occur without alcohol being involved. Drinking, though, may make it worse.

Myth 3. Only poor people hit their wives or partners.
Sorry. Wrong again. No one is immune — doctors, lawyers, wealthy businesspeople and celebrities — all have been guilty of domestic violence.

Myth 4. The woman did something to provoke it.
Wrong. Women have been beaten when they were sound asleep.

Myth 5. She likes it.
Yeah, right.

Myth 6. If the woman wanted to, she could leave.
Nope. Can the hostages in a hijacking leave?

Myth 7. Any man who would assault his family would harm other people too.
Not necessarily. The abuser gets away with it only because the violence is done in private.

Myth 8. At least a woman is safe when she's pregnant.
No way. Pregnant women are often abused.

Myth 9. It happens to other people.
Right, sure. If you're lucky.

WHY DOES IT HAPPEN?

Many things have allowed domestic violence to continue. Fortunately, people are thinking and talking about it a lot more these days. Think about the following:

• Lots of people grew up with violence in their own homes.

• Our society has conditioned women to be victims.

• People are afraid of breaking up the family.

• Sometimes women get blamed when they speak up.

• In the past, there was not much community support for women who did leave abusive husbands.

• Lacking finances, women had nowhere to go; the husband earned all the money.

• No one punished the men even when they were caught in the act.

Is it any wonder that the women caught in a cycle of violence find it hard, if not impossible, to leave? This has become known as the "battered wife syndrome." The phrase means that, after a while, a woman is so worn down that, psychologically, she cannot leave. She feels trapped. She may try to leave but she gets drawn back, over and over again. There have been situations where women have been assaulted over 200 times before getting up the nerve and strength to leave.

WHY DO MEN DO IT?

There are many reasons, but these are often mentioned by experts:

• Society has tolerated the violence.

• Men have been taught to solve problems by violent acts instead of by thinking or negotiating.

• Society often blamed the female victims as much as the men who assaulted them, so the men did not think it was their fault.

• Men who are violent have what is known as "poor impulse control." (Translation: They lose it easily.)

Guys who are violent toward their families tend to have very low self-esteem. They blame everyone else for their problems, are not very flexible and tend to be traditional in male-female relations. I also find that they tend to be real "B.S. artists"— by that I mean they can be charming liars.

WHAT CAN YOU DO?

On a practical level there are a few things that you can do to protect yourself and your family. Start with these:

• Educate your family. Have them read this chapter or *Surviving Your Divorce*, the other book that I wrote. It has a chapter on domestic violence too. Then, support your mom as she tries to deal with it. Be understanding of the situation your mom is in. Your family didn't get to be that way overnight, so fixing the problem will take time.

• Call the police. They have experience in dealing with these situations. In an emergency, call 911 (if the service is available in your community). Look up the telephone number for the police and write it down and put it somewhere it's easy to find.

• Find a friend for support.

• Tell your family doctor. He or she may have some helpful suggestions. Or speak to a teacher at school — he or she will know how to help you.

• Urge your mom to find out if there are any shelters for battered women in your area. Your mom should also check the availability of social assistance and legal aid.

• Develop an escape route for emergencies.

• Your mom should set aside a little money for a taxi in case of an emergency. Pack your own suitcase with a spare set of clothes. Take all your important I.D. Tell your mom you're ready to go if violence happens again.

• Ask a lawyer about a restraining order or a peace bond. Both are legal tools to keep someone from bothering you.

• If you or your mom have been injured, you can sue for damages or apply to the Criminal Injuries Compensation Board for financial help.

Remember it is not your job to stop the violence. But you may be able to give your mom the support she needs and help her to find someone who can stop the violence.

WHAT ABOUT DAD?

It may sound like I have no sympathy for the man in this situation. After all, the man probably doesn't want to be like that. We might even be tempted to say, "It is just the way he was raised." That is probably true, since most abusive men come from violent homes. But I have to admit I do not have any sympathy for these men. They know perfectly well that they cannot beat up their co-workers, or anyone else outside the home, and get away with it. Why should it be any different at home? They know it is wrong — and they *must* stop.

   The good news is that there are courses that can be taken by these men to teach them how to control their anger. It takes a lot to admit that a person has this problem, but the only guy I have any sympathy for is the guy who goes on his own for this help. He shouldn't have to wait until he is caught, charged, convicted and then ordered to go by a judge. He should do it because he wants to change.

A NOTE FOR YOUNG WOMEN

If you are a young woman reading this chapter and you have a boyfriend who fits the description that I gave earlier, then this is for you. **Dump him. Dump him. Dump him.** (Translation: **Dump him** — fast.)

If you have a boyfriend who embarrasses you on purpose, who insults you, who belittles you and makes you feel worthless, who threatens you, hits you, slaps or shoves you, is jealous and possessive, then you must end the relationship immediately. It is a ticket to trouble. If you have a boyfriend who makes you watch pornography or forces you to do sexual things that you don't want to do, then get out of this relationship. There are many guys out there who would love to have someone decent like you for a girlfriend. Going without a boyfriend is better than being "contaminated" by someone who only wants to control you for his own purposes. You deserve better. Ask yourself why you would even be with such a guy in the first place. Did you learn a lousy lesson at home? Want to change? You can.

Yes, your boyfriend needs help and, yes, he should get it, but that is his problem. Take care of yourself first. There is probably someone reading this right now and thinking, "But my boyfriend is different. Sure he's not nice all the time... He wants to be good but he can't help it. I will change him." I hate to rain on your parade but it ain't gonna happen. Abusive guys don't change because of something you do. They are not the way they are because of you, and they will not be different because of you. In other words, you didn't make him and you won't unmake him. These guys change when *they* want to change. Be supportive — but from a distance. The same thing applies to a boyfriend as to a violent father — the man must decide to find a program on his own.

I remember a case in which I represented a young woman who had just made the break from an abusive relationship. When I interviewed her, she mentioned that her boyfriend had treated his previous girlfriend the same way. On a hunch, I checked the court files to see if that girl had ever taken the guy to court. It turned out that, not only had she taken him to court for abuse, but he was *married* to her. In the court file I read a statement by his wife that he had also abused a previous girlfriend. When I checked that court file, the same statements had been made.

This guy had abused *three women* in exactly the same way. How did he manage to pull it off? Basically, he followed the same pattern of lies and abuse. I wish we could hang a flashing sign on these guys, but we can't. You just have to keep your eyes open and run like hell at the first sign of the abusive pattern.

A NOTE FOR YOUNG GUYS

If you are a young guy reading this and you recognize yourself, or one of your friends, I am sorry. You probably don't like yourself very much when the violence happens. If your girlfriend read this and broke up with you, I am *not* sorry. Good for her. She is looking after herself. You should do the same thing. Think about why you behave the way that you do. Where did you learn all that stuff? Take responsibility for your actions. Speak to your family doctor, a teacher you trust or a guidance counsellor. There is help out there.

VIOLENCE AGAINST YOU

I know some kids are reading this and thinking not about their moms but about themselves. There are parents out there who treat their children with the same kind of abuse that I described above. They hit them, they scream at them, they belittle and embarrass them.

One day at the supermarket, I got in a big argument with a woman who kept twisting her little boy's ear to punish him for the smallest things. I wondered, "If she does that in public, what does she do in private?!" Emotional abuse and neglect can be just as harmful as a hit or a smack. I think no one should tolerate it. If we look the other way it will just continue.

What can you do if the violence is against you? Well, you are no different than anyone else. If you are being smacked around or abused at home, do not cover it up. Get help. Speak to someone that you can trust, like a teacher, a friend's parent, a doctor. There are lots of people out there who would love to help you take the first step.

Every community has Children's Aid agencies. They are community-based supports for families. They have social workers and other professionals who can help you. Look in the phone book to see if there is one near you. If you are worried that the call will break up your family then you should speak to someone confidentially to see what your choices are. I tell young people not to worry too much about the possibility of breaking up the family. First, if there is violence or abuse it must stop, and the only way it will stop is if someone intervenes. For your own safety, it may need to be done. Second, someone else may be aware of what is going on and, if they report it, then a break-up will happen anyway. Finally, it is better for the family to get help on its own rather than wait for something really bad to happen.

Let's compare two situations that I have seen. In the first case the father and mother were having a lot of trouble. One day the mother and the children called the Children's Aid and asked for advice. The social workers came to the house and suggested regular visits with a counsellor and a home worker. Over time, the family gradually got control of the situation. In the second case the situation was the exact opposite. The family struggled along with the violence until one night the father gave the mother a particularly awful beating. The police came and took the father to jail. The father was charged with assault and the mother had to spend time in the hospital. The children spent two weeks in a foster home until the mother was OK. It was too late for counselling or social workers.

It may well be better to speak up right away, rather than wait. There may be a local telephone number in your community that you can call for confidential advice. In many cases you do not have to give your name, they will just let you talk and ask questions. When you are ready to get help, they are ready for you. Check the local phone book for these numbers. It never hurts to talk to someone on the phone. Give it a try. You can make a difference in your own life and in your parents' lives. You may want to start by reading this chapter again.

11 GETTING ALONG AFTER THE DUST SETTLES: Stepfamilies and Other Challenges

I think that one of the most difficult things that a kid must do after his or her parents get divorced is to try to blend into a new stepfamily. It can be very tough to get used to the idea that your mother or father is going to have a new spouse around the house — and sometimes with that spouse's kids crowding up the place! And sometimes it seems to happen so fast. You are barely living on your own with your mom or dad and "wham!" new people are moving in.

In some cases, your parents may be getting married again. In other cases, they may decide to live common law for awhile. Whichever way it happens, a new family can be a real struggle. In this chapter I would like to spend some time looking at how stepfamilies come together and to offer some suggestions on how things can be made a little easier for the new stepparent, for the new stepkids and for you.

I also would like to spend some time talking about the challenges you may face when living with just one parent. After a divorce, many parents go through a long stretch of not having any close relationships with members of the opposite sex. Never mind

living with someone, for years they may not even go on a date!
They may just have no interest in getting involved with someone
new.

STEPFAMILIES

What is a stepfamily? It includes any combination of two families
or one family and a new husband or wife. So, if a woman has two
children and marries a man with one child and they all move in
together, that is a stepfamily. If the man that she marries has no
children, it is still a stepfamily. If the woman has no children and
the man has kids, it is a stepfamily. In one case that I know of, the
man and the woman each had joint custody of their children. This
meant that, depending on the day or the week, they could have
anywhere from two to five children running around the house. But
they loved the situation and it worked for them.

Actually, that may be the key — it worked for them. Stepfamilies can include any combination that works for the parents and
children involved.

Why are they called stepfamilies? In Old English terms "steop"
meant bereavement or grief over the death of someone. So when a
family described the child of someone who had died, they called
the child a "steop child." The term was shortened and used to
describe any child who had lost a parent and was being cared for
by a new parent.

People have been trying to find new expressions to describe
the combination of two families. "Merging" or "blending" have
been suggested, but I think they sound too mechanical. Let's stick
with stepfamily until someone comes up with a better term.

People who don't know much about stepfamilies sometimes
have a reaction like "Poor kids, that family is not as 'good' as a
'natural family.' That family is really just two 'broken' families." I
guess we will just have to be patient and wait for such people to
catch up with the rest of us. By the year 2000 one out of every
three Canadian children will have spent some time living in a stepfamily. That is a lot of Canadian children. Stepfamilies are common
and "natural." They can be as strong as nonstepfamilies, if not
stronger.

Stepfamilies face challenges that nonstepfamilies do not. There are all those extra aunts, uncles, grandparents and cousins suddenly in the picture. And, don't forget, if your other parent gets remarried, the family can expand again, like a giant web. You may need a chart to keep track of them all.

Another challenge that these families face is the need for patience in developing relationships. In my own family, I had an older sister and a younger brother. It never occurred to me that I had a "choice" about getting to know them and building a relationship. They were just *there*. But all the stuff that families take for granted, stepfamilies need to think about. New brothers and sisters need to get to know each other. Don't forget that the stepparents are still building their love and relationship too. The key is to be patient and to give someone new the benefit of the doubt as the new family grows together.

If you have been on your own with your mom or dad for a long time, privacy and time together may seem rare with new kids running around. Be patient — your relationship is never in doubt. If you treat the new kids as equals and respect the fact that they are probably feeling the same way about you, then you will start to see them as new, lifelong friends. Respect their privacy needs and they will respect yours.

The new relationship that will be of most interest to you, of course, will be the new stepparent who has arrived on the scene. This parent may be under a lot of pressure. He or she is trying to build a relationship with your mom or dad and you at the same time. So the person may work too hard at trying to be nice. I remember one case where the new parent was a woman, Kate, who had never been married before and had never had children. She married a man who had three children. Two of them were in their teens and one was ten. She decided that she was going to be the best "mom" that these kids had ever seen. She was all over them — involved in all of their school stuff, volunteering for sports activities and entertaining like crazy.

The other thing that Kate decided to try her hand at was disciplining the children. She would give chores to the kids and would take away privileges if they didn't do the chores she had assigned to them. That was the way her parents had done it. She had hated it when she was a kid but, hey, it seemed to work. Besides, she didn't know any other method.

The father of the kids said that this was OK because he didn't want to handle discipline anyway. He felt he had enough to do just keeping the enlarged household going.

Kate did so much because she loved the kids' dad, and she wanted the kids to love her. And they could have; she was a great person. But they didn't. Instead, they tore her to pieces. Anything she tried to do for them was thrown back at her. She was blamed for the father's divorce even though she had never even met him until years after he had separated. There were days when the kids would act like she wasn't even in the room. Kate spent more than a few nights crying. The marriage suffered too.

But, to Kate's credit, she stuck it out. After years of terrible behaviour and some counselling for the family, the "children" (all now in university), realized what she was trying to do and decided to accept her. They finally treat her like a friend. They sure missed out at first, though.

Kate told me that if she had to do it all over again she would be a little more patient and not come on so strong. She realized that by trying to be the best mom ever she was implying that she was better than their natural mom. The kids were saying back to her, "No way!" But all of this hidden talk was in action, not words.

Kate also realized that the biggest mistake she had made was trying to discipline the kids on her own. There was no way she should have taken on that duty. The most she should have done was to provide little reminders about things that needed to be done. The kids' father should have looked after the serious discipline.

I think it is understandable for a kid to resist the control of a new stepparent. The new parent needs to build up his or her "right to authority" before trying to control the children. Once the children trust that parent, then the discipline can follow — in small amounts.

How can you avoid some of these problems in a stepfamily?

• Talk to your parent and the new parent about your feelings and your worries — be honest.

• Be patient and take the time to get to know the new parent and any children who join the family.

- Stay in touch with the rest of your family. Don't forget that all those aunts, uncles, cousins, grandparents and others are still thinking about you. If there was something that you used to do with them as a sort of tradition, then try to keep doing it.

- Resist the temptation to blackmail or negotiate extra privileges. Don't take advantage of the fact that the new parent is trying to get you to like him or her.

- Start doing something new that only your stepfamily does together. Call it the "new tradition."

- Don't tolerate any bad talk about your other parent. If your step-dad starts saying something about your natural dad, just speak right up, "I don't want to hear you saying bad things about...it makes me unhappy."

- Don't panic every time the new family hits a bump. *All families* have problems from time to time.

Just be patient and respectful and you won't go wrong. Give your new stepparent and stepfamily a chance and you might be pleasantly surprised.

SINGLE-PARENT FAMILIES

Let's look at the opposite situation. What if your mom or dad never remarry, never have new partners and you have them all to yourself? Sounds great, right? Well it can be, but you have to be careful sometimes. Let's look at some of the pitfalls.

We know from the chapter dealing with support that the financial situation can be rough for a while after separation. Two homes must sometimes survive on the money from one salary.

A pitfall that you must avoid is having your mom or dad lean on you as their *only* friend. You are a kid, your parent is an adult. It is great to be friends with your parent, even best friends, but not the only friend. I have seen situations where a mom was very heartbroken after her divorce. She had custody of the kids and the dad got remarried very quickly. She couldn't imagine being married again so she accepted that she would be single for the rest of her life.

The woman's daughter thought this was great for the first little while, then she noticed that her mom was relying very heavily on her for company. She felt bad about going on a sleepover because her mom would be alone for the night! Now that was going too far. The mom was dependent on the child.

The reverse can be common too. A child may cling to the custodial parent. This child would never think of going on a sleepover because he or she would be away from mom or dad for too long. For a young child that might be understandable, but not for an older kid.

Neither of these problems can be solved overnight but both the parents and the older children have to remember that a full life includes lots of friends and activities. Keep your life as rich and full as possible.

Some final words about the single parent. Some parents say that they will never marry again, and they say that they will never get involved. But I believe they all hope that love will come again into their lives. They want this for themselves and as your parent. They may well imagine a stepfamily for you. So, if that special someone comes along (there may be false alarms, so be patient) be supportive. If it looks like they are getting serious, you may want to reread the above section on stepfamilies and recall my advice about patience and respect.

It can be tough adjusting to all these changes in your life, but don't forget there are thousands of kids going through the same thing. Remember those statistics, one out of every three kids will live in a stepfamily sometime and, in Canada, 75,000 kids a year are affected by their parents' divorce. You are definitely not alone. Other kids have made it through and you will too.

12 MARRIAGE CONTRACTS AND OTHER AGREEMENTS

You have probably heard about marriage contracts or what some American TV shows refer to as "prenuptial agreements." In this chapter I would like to spend some time looking at three kinds of contracts that people can sign and that may have an important effect on families.

Your first reaction may be to wonder why someone would need a contract to cover something like being married or living together or fathering a child. Well, in Canada, people are allowed to put all kinds of things in contracts and in some cases the law even encourages them to do so. A little thinking ahead of time can save a lot of grief later. So let's look at each kind of contract and the things that people usually put in them.

MARRIAGE CONTRACTS

If two people are married to each other or planning on getting married, they can agree to set out in a contract some rules for what should happen while they are married. At the same time, they can guard against what might happen if, at a later date, they decide to get divorced.

I had a young couple approach me one day and ask if I would draft a marriage contract for them. They were going to get married in about three months and had planned the whole wedding. Then one night, when they were talking about their lives together, they each started to ask "What ifs?" They took turns saying, for example, "What if...we have children? Will we share the work of looking after them?" or "What if one of us quits his or her job to stay home and look after the kids?" or "What if we split up, would you want to have half of the family heirlooms that I inherited from my great-great-great-grandmother?" or "What if we split up after I had inherited my father's dairy farm, would you want half?" or "What if we have kids and we split up, who would get custody?" You can see what I am getting at here — an hour of these kinds of questions and they had scared the daylights out of each other.

They came to see me to try and settle some of these problems by agreeing in advance how disagreements in the marriage would be solved if they came up. They both swore that they loved each other and would never split up (it was like some kind of love song) but they would always add, "But what if...?" So I said, "Every couple that gets married or lives together is in love with each other, just like you two. But the smart couples set up a marriage contract to handle the 'what ifs' and the others have to pray that nothing ever goes wrong. Why not be smart?"

I started by explaining to them that a marriage contract — to be binding — has to be in writing, signed by both of them and witnessed. With a couple of exceptions, they could put anything they wanted into the agreement.

Right away they wanted to know what the exceptions were. I said that, really, there were only two they had to worry about. First, they could not decide in a marriage contract about what would happen to children if the marriage ends. That means they couldn't decide that one of them would have custody if they split up. Canadian laws, and our courts, do not think it is right to let important things affecting custody and access of children be put into contracts. The decisions made might not be the best ones for the children later on. This couple was not even married yet. The children might not be born for a few years. If the couple separated five years after that, who knows what would be best for the kids then? So, the rule is, in a marriage contract, you cannot agree to custody, access or child support. If you try to do it anyway, the court will just ignore that part of the contract.

The couple then asked me about child care while they were married — they assumed that the same rule would apply to that situation. (I think the woman was worried that she would get stuck doing all the diaper changing and that her husband would not be involved in child care like he should.) I had to explain that the rule was different if they were agreeing on how to raise their children. If they wanted to agree on diaper changing and child care or what school the children would go to or what religion they would practice, that would be fine. They could certainly put that in the contract.

I also explained that they could also put in anything about property sharing or keeping property separate, if that was what they wanted. We talked about the dairy farm and the heirlooms and other things. That's when the second exception came up. We began talking about the home they were going to live in after they were married. I explained that it would not matter who owned the home — it could be in the husband's name or it could be in the wife's name — each of them would be entitled to ask the court for permission to live in the house if they ever split up. I could see their eyes kind of spinning around because that's a little confusing. So I used an example.

"Let's say that the house is in your husband's name and that you live together for ten years, but you start to have problems. Let's say that your husband then threatens to throw you, the wife, out of the house because he says he owns it."

The husband jumped out of his chair and said, "Honey, I would never throw you out!"

"Whoa!" I said, "It is only an example!"

After he calmed down, I continued. "The court would not let you throw her out, even if she had agreed to it in a marriage contract." That is the other exception: a husband or wife cannot give up their right to possession of the family home at separation.

Aside from that, a couple can agree on anything. For example, they could agree that if the marriage ended in divorce neither of them would claim support from the other one, or that everything the woman owned before the marriage would continue to be hers if they split up. I explained that a marriage contract was really a

way of setting up a private system for running a marriage or for settling things if there was a separation.

Another important situation in which a couple might want to
consider a marriage contract is in the case of a second marriage.
Your parents may well be in this situation a few years after divorce.
I have often been consulted by men and women who have already
been married and divorced. They know what it's like to argue
about support and property division. When they meet someone
new and start to think about wedding bells, they often start thinking about a way to avoid all that stuff. They go into the second marriage a little wiser, shall we say.

I once prepared a contract for a woman named Lucy. Lucy had kept
the house from her first marriage. It had been a real struggle for her to
pay an expensive mortgage and raise the children all by herself, but she
did it. Then, out of the blue, she met a nice man named Tom, and she
decided that maybe marriage wasn't such a bad idea. She remembered,
though, from her first divorce that a home can be divided equally no
matter who owns it or paid for it.

I will never forget when she asked me, "Do you mean that if I
marry Tom and we get a divorce years from now, he will get a share
of the house even if I was the one who worked so hard to pay off
the mortgage...?" Her voice got a little higher and strained as she
asked the question.

"Whoa!" I said. "You're right, it would ordinarily be shared. But
not if you put in a marriage contract that the house is yours and
yours alone."

She started to feel a little better. It also turned out that Tom had
some things that he was worried about, so we put all of the
answers and protections in a contract. We ended up developing a
marriage contract for the two of them.

COHABITATION AGREEMENTS

Another kind of contract that couples sometimes sign is called a
cohabitation agreement. This is a marriage contract for people who
are going to live together but have decided not to get married. The
same exception about children applies to cohabitation agreements
— a couple cannot agree years in advance to custody, access or
child support.

The rule about possession of the home does not apply to cohabitation agreements because, as I discussed in the earlier chapter on property division, common-law couples have very few property rights. Possession of the home at separation is not one of them.

Before going on to talk about paternity agreements, I just want to mention a couple of things. First, people sometimes sign these kinds of agreements — marriage and cohabitation — *after* they are married or living together. In a couple of cases, people signed the contracts as a condition of getting back together. In other words, they split up and were going to stay separated but then, after talking to their lawyers, they agreed to get back together on certain conditions. The conditions were usually related to the problems they were having in the marriage.

Sometimes a couple are married and happy and they still need a marriage contract. I have seen situations where the husband was made a partner in a business and his partners insisted he have a marriage contract with his wife. In the contract the wife agrees not to claim the husband's share of the business if they should ever divorce. I mention this only because I didn't want you to think that your parents' marriage is in trouble just because they are talking about a marriage contract. It could just be related to a business deal.

It is best to have a lawyer when preparing or signing contracts like these. There have been cases where one person tricked the other person into signing away more than he or she thought or one partner lied about his or her property or misled the other person in some way. If the court finds out that a contract was signed only because of dishonesty, lying or a mistake, the judge will just wipe it out and refuse to enforce it. So a person should always get a lawyer's advice before signing a marriage or cohabitation agreement.

PATERNITY AGREEMENTS

This type of agreement is very unusual. In it, a person — a man — agrees that he is the father of a particular child.

The need for this type of agreement usually comes about because a man and a woman had sex, the woman became pregnant and then they argued about whether the man is really the father of the child. If he is the father, then they need to decide how much time, if any, he will spend with the child and how much child support he will pay as the child grows up.

If there is an argument about whether the man is the father, the matter can be settled with blood tests or DNA samples. When these tests are done, scientists compare the blood or DNA of the mother, the father and the child. If it matches, then the court will order that the father pay child support.

I had a case involving a young man who was accused of being the father of the next-door neighbour's grandchild. The young man's mother and father were visiting the neighbours when a baby, the grandchild, was also visiting. When the young man's mother commented on how beautiful the baby was, the neighbour said, "Well she should be, your son is the father!"

There was a little bit of excitement over that announcement. The young man, who was still in high school, swore that he was not the father. He admitted to me that he had, in fact, had sex with the neighbour's daughter, but it was only once and, well, nobody could get pregnant...if they only did it once, right? WRONG! He was the father.

The young man signed a paternity agreement and agreed that, as soon as he finished high school, he would start to pay some financial support for the child. I figure that he will pay about $100,000 in child support because of that one time.

There is an obvious moral to the story. Do you think that something like that could happen to you? Maybe you could be the girl who got pregnant? Maybe you could be the young man who has a $100,000 debt waiting for him when he graduates from high school? OK, so you're too smart to let anything like that happen. Let's just say I warned you.

People use marriage contracts, cohabitation agreements and paternity agreements to make private arrangements that will affect their families. I think we will be seeing more and more of them in years to come.

13 SOME PAGES TO HELP TO HELP WORK THINGS OUT

MY PLAN FOR MY FAMILY

My name is: _____   My age is: _____

My brothers and sisters are:

1. _____   age: _____

2. _____   age: _____

3. _____   age: _____

My mom is: _____

My dad is: _____

We have these pets:

1. _____

2. _____

3. _____

Other important family members are:

1. _____

2. _____

3. _____

Other important friends are:

1. _____

2. _____

3. _____

If I could talk to anyone about this it would be:

_____

The things I worry about in the split-up are: _____

_____

_____

The things I hate are: _____

_____

_____

I wish that my parents could: _____

_____

_____

These are important to me: _____

_____

_____

Things might be better if: _____

_____

_____

If I could have one wish after the divorce it would be: _____

_____

Signed this _____ day of _____ , 199—

_____

MY FEELINGS

1. *How are you feeling about this stuff?*

Circle the emotions that seem closest.

I feel:

ANGRY	RELIEVED	BLAMED
TRAPPED	LONELY	NERVOUS
WORRIED	STUCK	AFRAID
SHAKY	SAFE	HURT
IGNORED	MIXED UP	EMBARRASSED

2. *Why do you feel like that?*

Consider the emotions you circled and try to write down why you feel that way.

_____

_____

_____

_____

_____

_____

_____

SOME SUGGESTIONS THAT MIGHT HELP

DO:

Have a good cry.

Go for a walk.

Play your favourite game, sport or hobby.

Tell a friend how you feel.

Talk to a favourite aunt, uncle or grandparent.

Read a book.

Be extra nice to somebody.

Draw some pictures about your feelings.

Write a private journal.

Listen to your favourite music.

Remember — it will get better.

DO NOT:

Run away from home. (Everyone will worry and you'll just have to come back.)

Fight with your friends or brothers and sisters. (They feel bad too.)

Yell and scream at people. (They'll think you're nuts!)

Sulk and refuse to talk to anyone. (People need to know what you want.)

Quit your favourite sport or hobby. (Hey, they're fun. Why quit?)

Drink and smoke. (Like, you need another reason not to?)

Eat like a pig! (It never helps.)

Starve yourself. (You'd be crazy. There's too much good stuff.)

Try to fix the situation by yourself. (That's for the adults.)

Hate your mom or dad. (They are hurting, too.)

Smash or vandalize stuff. (It's a crime, for one thing, and it may just make matters worse.)

Give your teachers a hard time. (They may be able to help, if you talk to them.)

Just remember, the things that are upsetting you are not your fault. Hopefully, the adults who caused the problem are working to fix things in a way that meets your needs as well as their own. I know it probably seems pretty bad and you probably think it will never get better, but trust me — it *will* get better. You just have to be patient. (Boy, do I ever sound like a parent sometimes or what?)

Questions? Thoughts? Comments? Things you need?
Try to take some time and use some separate pages to write down or draw whatever is on your mind.

Try writing a letter to your mom or dad about how you feel or what you want and need.

If you could write a letter to the judge, what would you say?

14 SO YOU'D LIKE TO BE A LAWYER?

If you've read this far, you now know more about family law than most people, including your parents. Why not think about becoming a lawyer? You have probably heard people make jokes about lawyers (usually mean ones) or you have heard people talk about lawyers like they have some kind of special power. Well, the truth is — as usual — somewhere in between. I think the jokes got started for a couple of reasons. Lawyers often charge a lot of money for the work that they do, and nobody likes to spend money unless it is for a good reason. So I think that people sometimes resent the fact that lawyers charge so much. But added to this is the fact that, when people use lawyers, it is because the people have problems that are already making them unhappy. The lawyer is right in the middle of all the unhappiness. This can make it a tough job.

That is one side of being a lawyer — the teasing and the jokes. Another side is the way people treat you once they find out that you are a lawyer! Wow! It is like you are supposed to know everything about everything. Once they forget about the jokes, it is amazing how people really listen to your opinion — even when it is not about the law. This is because the kind of work that a lawyer

does often brings him or her into contact with all kinds of interesting problems. One day, a lawyer may be working on a case
about a car accident in which people were injured. The next day,
he or she may be working on a case about a woman who wants to
start a new company to manufacture the latest type of computer
software. Every day there's something new and different. The
training we receive in law school prepares us to deal with all kinds
of situations.

I think that I enjoy being a lawyer for several reasons. The work
is very interesting, you get to meet lots of interesting people, many
of whom are involved in interesting work (you don't just meet
criminals) and, since every case is different, you learn something
new every day. You have a chance to help people who are in trouble and need your special knowledge. Your training allows you to
think of ways to improve our society. And, let's not forget, you can
make a good living as a lawyer.

So, how do you get to be a lawyer? It helps if you like school
because there is a lot of studying involved. When I was in Grade 9
I was not a very good student. I was more interested in playing
football and other sports than working at my school studies. One
day a very good teacher took a few minutes to work with me on a
book report and I realized that the book was interesting and that I
felt good about what I was learning. That teacher later showed me
how to study. I was in Grade 9 and I didn't know that there was a
way to study that made the work fun. After he helped me, my
grades went up and I loved school. It was around that time that I
started to like writing and got interested in law. Years later I still
think back about that teacher (Mr. Harwood, where are you?). I
wonder what would have happened to me if he had not been there
for me.

Let's start by explaining the steps that you must go through to
become a lawyer. You do not have to decide in Grade 7 or 8 or
even in high school that you want to be a lawyer. Also, don't get
me wrong, there are many good careers that will allow you to help
people and enjoy your work. Law is just one. But assuming that you
think you might like to head in that direction, you will definitely
need to finish high school. There is no need to concentrate on sci-
ences or math or history. You just need to concentrate on developing good study habits.

Try to learn about as many areas as possible while you're in school, because then you will discover the area that you love the most. If you never read about how buildings are made, you will never know if you might want to be an architect. Read everything — good and bad. If you don't read the occasional piece of junk for fun, then you might not appreciate all the really good books out there.

Don't ignore a subject because you think it is boring or because you don't like it or because you think it will be too hard. A couple of years ago I finally admitted that I was a little afraid of — this is embarrassing — motorcycles. I could drive a car, but I just thought I could not operate a motorcycle. Anyway, I did not want to avoid motorcycles all my life, so I went back to school and took a course on how to drive a motorcycle. I now have my biker licence!

If you confront your fears, you usually find out that there was nothing to be afraid of in the first place. I mention this for a reason. Learning and studying will consume a lot of your time and energy throughout your lifetime — especially if you want to be a lawyer. The learning never stops, so you should learn to enjoy it.

After high school you will need to go to university. The first three or four years are known as "undergraduate" and will give you a chance to try many different areas of study. It is very important to work hard and to get good grades during these first three years of university; otherwise, you'll never get into law school. Every year there are thousands of very bright people who try to get into law school, but only a small percentage are accepted. How do law schools decide whom to accept? Grades! If you did well in your undergraduate courses, then you will have a good chance. The law schools, which are part of a university, also look at the results of a special exam that you must write in order to apply. It is called the Law School Aptitude Test (LSAT).

But the hard work is just beginning. Next you must spend three years in law school. Each year you will study different areas of law — criminal law, medical law, international law, space law, environmental law, the law of contracts and so on. As you study you will find certain parts of the law that you really like.

After three years of studying and exams, you get a chance to go out and work for a year as a student with a law firm. You actually get paid to study! This is called "articling." It is really like being an apprentice. After the year of work you get an unusual reward — you get to go back to school for several more months to polish your learning. If you pass that last stage, usually called the bar admission course, then you are "called to the bar" as a lawyer.

After all that, you are entitled to go out and offer your special knowledge to the public. This is called practising law. You're a lawyer! It's a job you can really take pride in. Then someone will start telling a lawyer joke and you will want to belt them! But you won't, because that would be a crime. You would have to hire a lawyer...and we now know how expensive that can be.

I hope that some of you reading this chapter will consider becoming a lawyer. For all the joking and mean stuff that is said about lawyers, it is still a great career.

Good luck...I hope we have a case together some day.

15 WRAPPING UP: The Top Ten Things to Remember

Give yourself a pat on the back if you read most or all of the book. It's not easy to work through so much stuff, especially when it is emotional and affects your own family. Just in case you forgot some of the more important points, I thought it might be helpful to wrap up with a summary, sort of "The top ten things kids should remember after reading this book."

Let's do this like they do on TV, counting backwards:

10. Don't get dragged into message delivery between your parents, especially, "Mom said to tell you ..." "Dad said to tell you ..." Avoid the blaming that may go on. Just say to your parent, "That is between you and Mom/Dad. I don't want to hear about it. Talk to her/him." Tell your parent more than once if you have to. Show him or her this book, to back you up.

9. Remember that, financially, things will likely be different after the separation. The property that your parents bought during their marriage, as well as their debts, must be divided. Support, both spousal and child, is supposed to help the parent with

custody meet expenses. Child support may have to be paid until you are in university (18, 19 or 20 years old). Spousal support can vary, but is used to help meet a parent's expenses until he or she can get a job and be financially independent. If the parent in need is older or has no skills or is ill, then spousal support can go on indefinitely.

8. There is absolutely no excuse for violence in your home — whether against you, your brothers or sisters or your parents. If it happens, speak to someone you trust, like a teacher, a family member or your family doctor. There are people out there who can help. Call the police if you have to. They have experience dealing with angry parents who are arguing with each other.

7. The only difference between the way common-law spouses and legally married spouses are treated when they separate is in the division of their property and debts. Custody, access and support are figured out the same way. Property and debt division is much more complicated for common-law couples. Each person must prove why he or she is entitled to share in any particular piece of property. When you are legally married it is assumed that each spouse has a share in every piece of property.

6. Now that you understand all this stuff — SPEAK UP! Let your parents know what you think. Let them know what you want. Let them know what you expect from both of them. Let them know what you are worried about. Let them know that you are relying on them to make decisions that are best for you and your brothers and sisters.

5. Custody, access, shared parenting, coparenting, joint custody — there is a lot of room for flexibility in having time with your parents. The decision is supposed to be based on what is in *your* best interests. Let them know that you expect them to be creative in designing a way for you to see and remain in contact with both parents. So, go back and read point number 6.

4. Find a friend for support, somebody who will listen and talk with you about all this. Sometimes it helps to think out loud with someone you trust. And don't forget to have some fun. It seems awful sometimes, but the situation will get better. Blow off some steam if

you need to! Hit, kick, smash, clobber, pound — a ball (not people). It will feel great. Do not be afraid to ask for help if pounding a ball doesn't seem to be enough.

3. Don't forget — divorce ends your parents' legal marriage, not their jobs as mother and father.

2. Now that you understand the situation and now that you have spoken up, let the people who made the problems be the ones to fix them. You are not supposed to look after everyone or solve the problems. Let the adults do it.

1. I think you probably know what I am going to say — *It is not your fault.* Lots of things cause people to separate or divorce; *you* are not one of them. Thousands of kids have survived divorce and you will too. I just hope that by reading this book it will be easier for you.

Good luck. I will be thinking about you.
Mike

APPENDIX I
Common Questions
and Answers

In this section of the book I have collected the common questions that young people ask me about divorce and separation.

Q. Why? Why does it happen? Why my family? Why now?

A. We might as well deal with as many "whys" as possible. It may not be helpful to you specifically, but there are no one-size-fits-all answers to the question why. Divorce hits almost one out of every three marriages in Canada. It can be caused by a lot of things, including the fact that people change and fall out of love with each other. Remember parents fall out of love with each other — not their children. In some cases marriage problems are caused by financial strain. In other cases they are caused by illness (mental or physical), including alcoholism, drugs or gambling. It can happen to any family at any time. Marriage problems always have something to do with the adults and never, in my experience, have anything to do with the children. Children do not cause divorces.

Q. Why is everyone acting so weird? One minute they are depressed, the next minute they are angry, and the next they are acting like nothing is wrong. What am I supposed to do?

A. There may not be much that you can do while your parents are on an emotional roller coaster. They will go through many different phases — anger, denial, depression, false hopes and — finally — acceptance. These are normal feelings for people who are trying to cope with something that hurts them very much. They are also worried about how a divorce will affect you. Give them time, be patient. Do not try to rescue your parents. You didn't put them in this state of mind, so you cannot get them out. Don't think that you can fix things by being "extra good."

Q. How long does it take to get this over with?

A. The feelings may last for a long time, but the separation and divorce process doesn't usually last more than two or three years. The judge, in most cases, will not order a divorce until one year of separation has passed. In the meantime, your parents may start to try to work out the main disagreements, with their lawyers acting as negotiators. A divorce can be wrapped up quickly if everyone agrees. But sometimes that takes a while.

Q. What are my parents talking about with those lawyers?

A. Your parents need to work out at least six things: custody, access, child support, spousal support, property division and the divorce itself. Some things, like the divorce grounds, may be settled quickly. Other things, like custody and property division, can go on for a longer time.

Q. Do they both need lawyers?

A. Very few people going through a divorce can afford not to have their own lawyer. The issues are serious. Yes, each parent needs a good, experienced family law lawyer. They should both shop around until they find someone with whom they are comfortable.

Each will need his or her own lawyer; they can't share one. The law society in each province can refer them to experienced family law lawyers.

Q. How much will the lawyers cost?

A. Lawyers charge by the hour for their advice — anywhere from $150 to $350. A day in court can cost over $2,000 for each lawyer. The faster everyone agrees, the less expensive it will be. Sometimes a person may be able to get legal aid (government-paid legal advice), but not always.

Q. What will happen to me?

A. Your parents will be discussing who will have responsibility for you and your brothers and sisters. They need to decide quite a few things — where you will live from day to day and who should make all the major decisions that concern you, such as school, health and maybe religion.

Your parents may agree to share decision making and their time with you. This is called "joint custody." If you will live with one parent and see the other one from time to time, then one will have custody and the other will have access. Most parents will also want to sort out things like holidays, birthdays, and so on.

Q. Will I have a say?

A. Yes. If you are older than 9 or 10, and mature enough, then your opinion will count. You need to be honest about what you think is best for you and what you want. Most importantly, you have to speak up!

Q. What about support? Who will pay? What should I do?

A. Your parents will have to agree on the support that is to be paid. Some of that support will be paid for you; some may be spousal support. Other than that you don't need to think about it. I suggest that you leave all the financial stuff to your parents. If they start to talk to you about support, politely tell them that it is between the adults and not for the children to sort out.

Q. Same thing for property?

A. Yup.

Q. My mom and dad never got married. Will that make a difference?

A. Yes, in some ways. First, they won't need a divorce; they just start living apart. Second, they don't use the same rules that married people do for property division. They must prove ownership of everything to which they think they are entitled. It is more difficult in some ways for common-law couples to divide their property. If they were married the law would tell them how to divide it by using a formula. But you don't need to worry about that stuff; that's for the adults.

Q. Can I have my own lawyer?

A. Yes. In many provinces the court will sometimes order that children have their own lawyers. This lawyer won't cost you anything and he or she is supposed to tell the court what you want. So be honest with your lawyer if one is appointed for you.

Q. My parents have been arguing a lot and I'm afraid that my mom could get hurt. What should I do?

A. In an emergency, dial 911 or the local police number. Police are trained to help in such cases. If you are just worried, talk to a teacher, a friend, a relative whom you trust or even your family doctor.

Q. Does everything have to go to court? Do I have to be a witness?

A. No. Most of the time parents can work things out without going to court. It may take time to find the right agreement, but most of them do. It would be very unusual for a child to be a witness in a divorce or family law case. The judge will tell the parents to do just about anything to avoid having a child give evidence. Your lawyer should be able to tell the judge anything important that needs to be passed on.

APPENDIX II
Legal Papers to Consider

In this part of the book I thought you might like to see some of the legal papers involved in family law. We have discussed Petitions for Divorce and Marriage Contracts and Separation Agreements, so here is what they, and some other documents, actually look like:

1. A Petition for Divorce
2. A Divorce Judgment
3. Domestic Contracts

    (a) A Separation Agreement

    (b) A Marriage Contract (or what some people call Prenuptial Agreements)

4. A Financial Statement

1. A PETITION FOR DIVORCE

The requirements for a divorce are set out in the federal *Divorce Act*. The standards are therefore the same in every province and territory. The Petition is the formal document that starts the divorce case's journey through the legal system. It is prepared in the lawyer's office, signed by the person asking for the divorce (the petitioner) and his or her lawyer, issued at the courthouse (meaning it is checked over by court staff and authorized by them to proceed) and then served on the other spouse (the respondent). Whether the divorce is contested, uncontested or a joint petition for divorce, it is always started by petition, and it ends with a judgment. For more information see Chapter 4, "Divorce," and the definition in the Glossary.

Two documents are reproduced here:

Petition for Divorce

Joint Petition for Divorce

(Note that the symbol ">" means "insert appropriate information here.")

Court File No.1234/99

ONTARIO COURT OF JUSTICE (GENERAL DIVISION)

B E T W E E N :

>

PETITIONER
(HUSBAND)

and

>

RESPONDENT
(WIFE)

PETITION FOR DIVORCE

TO THE RESPONDENT

A LEGAL PROCEEDING FOR DIVORCE HAS BEEN COM-MENCED AGAINST YOU by the petitioner. The claim made against you appears on the following pages.

IF YOU WISH TO DEFEND THIS PROCEEDING, you or an Ontario lawyer acting for you must prepare an answer in Form 69D prescribed by the Rules of Civil Procedure, serve it on the petitioner's lawyer(s) or, where the petitioner does not have a lawyer, serve it on the petitioner, and file it, with proof of service, in this court office, WITHIN TWENTY DAYS after this petition is served on you, if you are served in Ontario.

If you are served in another province or territory of Canada or in the United States of America, the period for servicing and filing your answer is forty days. If you are served outside Canada and the United States of America, the period is sixty days.

Instead of serving and filing an answer, you may serve and file a notice of intent to defend in Form 69J prescribed by the Rules of Civil Procedure. This will entitle you to ten more days within which to serve and file your answer.

If this petition for divorce contains a claim for support or a division of property, you must serve and file a financial statement in Form 69K prescribed by the Rules of Civil Procedure within the time set out above for serving and filing your answer, whether or not you wish to defend this proceeding. If you serve and file an answer, your financial statement must accompany your answer.

IF YOU FAIL TO SERVE AND FILE AN ANSWER, A DIVORCE MAY BE GRANTED IN YOUR ABSENCE AND WITHOUT FURTHER NOTICE TO YOU, JUDGMENT MAY BE GRANTED AGAINST YOU ON ANY OTHER CLAIM IN THIS PETITION AND YOU MAY LOSE

YOUR RIGHT TO SUPPORT OR DIVISION OF PROPERTY. IF YOU
WISH TO DEFEND THIS PROCEEDING BUT ARE UNABLE TO PAY
LEGAL FEES, LEGAL AID MAY BE AVAILABLE TO YOU BY CON-
TACTING A LOCAL LEGAL AID OFFICE.

NEITHER SPOUSE IS FREE TO REMARRY until a divorce has
been granted and has taken effect. Once a divorce has taken effect,
you may obtain a certificate of divorce from this court office.

Date   Issued by
                                                  Local registrar
                                        Address of court office
                                        >

CLAIM

1. The petitioner claims:

    (a) divorce;

    (b) under the Divorce Act *(Canada)*
         (i)

    (c) under the *Family Law Act,*
         (i)

GROUNDS FOR DIVORCE — SEPARATION

2. (a) The spouses have lived separate and apart since >.

The spouses have resumed cohabitation during the following
periods in an unsuccessful attempt at reconciliation:

Date(s) of cohabitation

GROUNDS FOR DIVORCE — ADULTERY

2. (b) The respondent spouse has committed adultery. Particulars are as follows:

GROUNDS FOR DIVORCE — CRUELTY

2. (c) The respondent has treated the petitioner with physical or mental cruelty of such a kind as to render intolerable the continued cohabitation of the spouses. Particulars are as follows:

RECONCILIATION

3. There is no possibility of reconciliation of the spouses.
4. The following efforts to reconcile have been made:

DETAILS OF MARRIAGE

5. Date of marriage:

6. Place of marriage:

7. Wife's surname immediately before marriage:

8. Wife's surname at birth:

9. Husband's surname immediately before marriage:

10. Husband's surname at birth:

11. Marital status of husband at time of marriage:

12. Marital status of wife at time of marriage:

13. Wife's birthplace:

14. Wife's birth date:

15. Husband's birthplace:

16. Husband's birth date:

17. (a) [ ] A certificate of   [ ] the marriage
                                    [ ] the registration of the marriage

   of the spouses has been filed with the court.

   (b) [ ] It is impossible to obtain a certificate of the marriage or
       its registration because:

   (c) [ ] A certificate of the marriage or its registration will be
       filed before this action is set down for trial or a motion is
       made for judgment.

RESIDENCE

18. The petitioner has resided in: _____ since

_____

19. The respondent has resided in: since _____ since

_____

20. The respondent's current address is: _____

_____

21. The [ ] petitioner
        [ ] respondent

has habitually resided in Ontario for at least one year immediately
preceding the commencement of this proceeding.

CHILDREN

22. The following are all the living children of the marriage as
defined by the Divorce Act (Canada):

Full name   Birth date   School and   Person with whom
grade or   child lives
year   and length of time
child has lived there

The children ordinarily reside in: _____

23. (a) The petitioner seeks an order for custody or joint custody
    of the following children on the following terms:

    Name of child   Terms of the order

    The respondent   [ ] agrees
    [ ] does not agree with the above terms.

    (b) The petitioner is not seeking an order for custody and
    [ ]   is content that a previous order for custody continue
    in force
    [ ]   is attempting to obtain an order for custody in another
    proceeding full particulars of which are as follows:

    (c) The petitioner seeks an order for access (visiting arrange
    ments) and is content that the petitioner have an order for
    custody of the following children on the following terms:

    Name of child   Terms of the order

    The respondent   [ ] agrees
    [ ] does not agree with the above terms.

24. (a) The following are the existing visiting arrangements
    (access) for the spouse who does not have the children living
    with him or her:

(b) The existing visiting arrangements (access) are
[ ] satisfactory
[ ] not satisfactory.

25. The order sought in paragraph 23 is in the best interests of the children for the following reasons:

26. The following material changes in the circumstances of the spouses are expected to affect the children, their custody and the visiting arrangements (access) in the future:

27. (a) The existing arrangements between the spouses for support for the children are as follows:

Amount paid	Time period (weekly, monthly, (etc.)	Paid by (husband or wife)	Paid for (name of child)

(b) The existing support arrangements
[ ] are being honoured.
[ ] are not being honoured.
(c) The petitioner proposes that the support arrangements for the children should be as follows:

Amount paid	Time period (weekly, monthly, (etc.)	Paid by (husband or wife)	Paid for (name of child)

28. The educational needs of the children [ ] are being met.
                                         [ ] are not being met.

OTHER COURT PROCEEDINGS

29. The following are all other proceedings with reference to the marriage or any child of the marriage:

DOMESTIC CONTRACTS AND FINANCIAL ARRANGEMENTS

30. The spouses have entered into the following domestic contracts and other written or oral financial arrangements:

Date   **Nature of contract**   **Status**
                  or arrangement

COLLUSION, CONDONATION AND CONNIVANCE

31. There has been no collusion in relation to this divorce proceeding.

32. There has been no condonation of or connivance at the grounds for divorce in this proceeding.

MATTERS OTHER THAN DIVORCE AND CUSTODY

33. The grounds for the relief sought in paragraph 1, other than a divorce or custody, are as follows:

TRIAL

34. The petitioner proposes that if there is a trial in this action, it be held at

DECLARATION OF PETITIONER

35. I have read and understand this petition for divorce. The statements in it are true, to the best of my knowledge, information and belief.

Date:_____

STATEMENT OF SOLICITOR

36. I,   , solicitor for the petitioner, certify to this court that I have complied with the requirements of section 9 of the *Divorce Act* (*Canada*).

Date: _____

Solicitors for the petitioner

STATEMENT OF WIFE'S SOLICITOR

33. I,   , solicitor for the wife, certify to this court that I have complied with the requirements of section 9 of the *Divorce Act (Canada)*.

I also certify that I have advised the wife that she has the right to seek independent legal advice and retain separate counsel in this proceeding.

Date _____   Signature of solicitor _____

Name, address and telephone number of solicitor

STATEMENT OF HUSBAND'S SOLICITOR

34. I,   , solicitor for the husband, certify to this court that I have complied with the requirements of section 9 of the *Divorce Act (Canada)*.

I also certify that I have advised the husband that he has the right to seek independent legal advice and retain separate counsel in this proceeding.

Date _____   Signature of solicitor _____
_____ *Name, address and telephone number of solicitor*

2. A DIVORCE JUDGMENT

Court File No. 1234

ONTARIO COURT
(GENERAL DIVISION)

THE HONOURABLE	)	MONDAY, THE 12
JUSTICE COCHRANE	)	DAY OF AUGUST, 1996

BETWEEN:

>

Petitioner
(HUSBAND)

and

>

Respondent
(WIFE)

DIVORCE JUDGMENT

THIS MOTION made by the petitioner for judgment for divorce was heard this day at Toronto, Ontario. The respondent did not defend this action although properly served with the petition as appears from the affidavit of service filed.

ON READING the petition, the notice of motion for judgment, the affidavit dated > of the petitioner filed in support of the motion,

1.   THIS COURT ORDERS AND ADJUDGES that > and >, who were married at > on >, are divorced and that the divorce takes effect on >

2.   THIS COURT ORDERS AND ADJUDGES, under the *Divorce Act (Canada)*, that > (custody, access, support and so on)

THIS JUDGMENT BEARS INTEREST at the rate of   percent per year commencing on

THE SPOUSES ARE NOT FREE TO REMARRY UNTIL THIS JUDGMENT TAKES EFFECT, AT WHICH TIME A CERTIFICATE OF DIVORCE MAY BE OBTAINED FROM THIS COURT. IF AN APPEAL IS TAKEN, IT MAY DELAY THE DATE WHEN THIS JUDGMENT TAKES EFFECT.

3. DOMESTIC CONTRACTS

    (a) A Separation Agreement
    (b) A Marriage Contract

(a) A SEPARATION AGREEMENT

The separation agreement is the most common of the three types of domestic contract (the other two are cohabitation agreements and marriage contracts). All three contracts must be written, signed and witnessed. A separation agreement acknowledges that the parties are living separate and apart and intend to do so from now on. It sets out important details about their background, their marriage, children and so on. It then describes, in as much detail as is required, the terms upon which the parties will end their marriage. It can deal with all or only some of the outstanding concerns. It may describe who will have custody and access, who will have which pieces of property, possession of the home on an interim or permanent basis, responsibility for family debts, life insurance and so on. The agreement can be final or interim (temporary). The following example of a separation agreement is not a complete document but shows a selection of typical provisions and some alternatives. Note that the symbol ">" means "insert appropriate information here." Law offices have draft clauses and agreements in their computers. Legal secretaries prepare a first draft by filling in the blanks. While the following is not necessarily a model agreement for your situation, it will help you to understand how comprehensive an agreement can be. References are made to certain Ontario laws.

THIS IS A SEPARATION AGREEMENT MADE ON >, 19>.

B E T W E E N :

The husband/father
- and -
The wife/mother

1. <u>INTERPRETATION</u>

(1) In this Agreement,

(a) "husband" means >, who is one of the parties to this Agreement, whether or not the husband and the wife are subsequently divorced;

(b) "wife" means >, who is one of the parties to this Agreement, whether or not the husband and the wife are subsequently divorced;

(c) "child" means >, born on >, or, >, born on >, both of whom are the children >who is the child> of the husband and the wife;

(>) "cohabit" means to live together in a conjugal relationship; whether within or outside marriage;

  >) "matrimonial home" means the buildings and lot located at >;

> (>) "cottage" means the buildings and lot called >;

(>) "Family Law Act" means the *Family Law Act*;

(>) "property" has the meaning given by the *Family Law Act*;

2. <u>BACKGROUND</u>

This Agreement is entered into on the basis of the following, among other facts:

(a) The parties were married at >, at >.

>(>) The parties have > child >: >, born on >, and >, born on >.>

>(>) The parties have no children and none are intended.>

>(>) The parties are living separate and apart from each other since >, and there is no reasonable prospect of their resuming cohabitation.

>(>) The parties desire to settle by agreement all their rights and obligations which they have or may have with respect to:

>(i) the custody of, and access to their child >,>

>(>) the support of their child >,>

>(>) possession, ownership and division of their property; and

>(>) support of each other.

3. <u>AGREEMENT</u>

Each party agrees with the other to be bound by the provisions of this Agreement.

4. <u>DOMESTIC CONTRACT</u>

Each party acknowledges that this Agreement is entered into under >s. 54 of the *Family Law Act* and is a domestic contract, which prevails over the same matters provided for in the Act or its successor.

5. <u>EFFECTIVE DATE</u>

This Agreement will take effect on the date it is signed by the last of the husband or the wife.

6. <u>LIVING SEPARATE AND APART</u>

The parties will live separate and apart from each other for the rest of their lives.

7. <u>FREEDOM FROM THE OTHER</u>

Neither party will molest, annoy, harass or in any way interfere with the other, or attempt to compel the other to cohabit or live with him or her.

>. <u>CUSTODY AND ACCESS</u>

(1) The wife will have custody of the child, subject to reasonable access by the husband on reasonable notice to the wife of his intention to exercise such access.

(>) The husband will have access to the child > as follows:

> (Be very specific: days, times, holidays, special events, total number of days per year, make-up times.)

(>) The husband and the wife each acknowledge that it is in the best interests of the child > for > to have frequent contact with > father and to spend time with him. Accordingly, the husband and the wife will each use their best efforts for the child > to have frequent and regular periods of access with the husband consisting of a combination of both daytime and overnight visits appropriate to the needs and stage of development of the child >.

(>) In making plans for access the husband and the wife will give the needs and convenience of the child > primary importance and will give their own needs and convenience only secondary importance.

(>) The parties will keep each other fully informed of all matters touching the interest of the child > and they will confer as often as necessary to solve any difficulty raised by or on behalf of the child.

>. <u>CUSTODY AND ACCESS (JOINT)</u>

(>) The child > shall be in the joint custody of the husband and the wife. The child > shall have > primary residence in the home of the child >.

(>) The husband and wife each acknowledge that the other is a devoted and loving parent. The > acknowledges that it is essential to the welfare of the child > that > have as close communication and contact with the > as is reasonably possible, commensurate with the best interests of the child >.

(>) The husband and wife agree and undertake that in all matters relating to the custody, maintenance, education and general well being of the child >, the child's > best interests and wishes shall at all times be paramount.

(>) The husband and wife shall conscientiously respect the rights of one another regarding the child >. The husband and wife shall continue to instill in the child > respect for both of > parents and grandparents, and neither the husband nor wife shall by any act, omission or innuendo, in any way tend or attempt to alienate the child > from either of them. The child > shall be taught to continue to love and respect both > parents.

(>) The husband and wife shall have the right to communicate with the child > by telephone and letter at all reasonable times, provided that such telephone communication shall not interfere with the private life of either the husband or the wife.

(>) The husband and wife agree that there shall be full disclosure between them in all matters touching the welfare of the child >, and they agree that they shall confer as often as necessary to consider any problem or difficulty or matter requiring consideration touching the welfare of the child >.

(>) The > shall have generous and regular access to the child >. It is acknowledged that the kind, frequency and duration of such access should be established in advance, and made as certain as existing circumstances permit, in order the enable the child >, the husband and the wife to make plans for their day-to-day living.

(>) If special occasions, holidays, excursions or other presently unforeseeable opportunities become available to the child >, neither the husband nor the wife will unreasonably insist that visiting arrangements be adhered to without exception. On the contrary, the husband and the wife shall at all times maintain a reasonable and flexible position respecting the visiting arrangements with the child >, and at all times, the best interests of the child > shall prevail.

(>) In any matter of contention between the husband and the wife which the husband and wife cannot resolve between themselves by mutual agreement, the parties agree to mediate any such disagreements or differences of opinion through a mediator that the parties may hereafter agree upon. If the parties are not able to agree on a mediator or if the mediation is unsuccessful the parties acknowledge that either one of them may bring an application to a court of competent jurisdiction to resolve the outstanding matters between them.

(>) The husband and wife acknowledge that the wife > may wish to change her > residence from the Province of [Ontario] as a result of remarriage or career opportunities. The husband > acknowledges that provided that the wife > is leaving the Province of [Ontario] for such reasons he > will not take any action that would prevent the wife > from leaving the Province of [Ontario] or unduly insist of exercising the access as set out in this agreement in order that the wife > be prevented from changing her residence from the Province of [Ontario]. The wife > agrees to give the husband > at least sixty (60) days notice of any intention to change her > residence from the Province of [Ontario] for the reasons set out in this paragraph so that the parties may make alternate arrangements with respect to access to the children, or

(>) Neither party shall move more than 30 km from the city of > without the consent of the other.

(>) Neither shall change the child's name without the consent of the other.

(>) FINANCIAL PROVISION

(>) Commencing on the > day of >, 199>, and on the > day of each and every month thereafter, the husband shall pay to the wife for the support of the child >, the sum of > per month <per child>, being a total of > for the support of >, until one or more of the following occurs:
   (i)   the child becomes eighteen years old and ceases to be in full-time attendance at an educational institution;
   (ii)   the child ceases to reside with the wife;
   (iii) the child becomes twenty-one years old;
   (iv)   the child marries; or
   (v)   the child dies.

(>) In clause > (ii), "reside" means to live in the home of the wife, and the child does not cease to reside in the home of the wife when the child is temporarily away from home to attend an educational institution, to work at summer employment, or to enjoy a reasonable holiday.

(>) Commencing on the > day of >, 19>, and on the > day of each and every month thereafter, the husband shall pay to the wife for her own support, the sum of > per month, until one or more of the following occurs:

(i)   the wife remarries or cohabits;

(ii)   the wife dies; or

(iii)   the husband dies.>

>. MATRIMONIAL HOME AND CONTENTS

(1) The parties acknowledge that they hold the matrimonial home as joint tenants.

>(>)The parties agree that the wife > may remain in exclusive possession of the matrimonial home until one or more of the following occurs:

(a) five years elapse from the date of this Agreement;

(b) the wife remarries;
(c) the wife cohabits with another man;

(d) the wife ceases to reside on a full-time basis in the premises;

(e) the husband and the wife agree in writing to the contrary.

(>) During the period of her > exclusive possession of the matrimonial home, the wife > will be responsible for paying all mortgage payments, taxes, insurance premiums, heating, water and other charges related to the matrimonial home, and will save the husband > harmless from all liability for those payments.

(>) The wife > will keep the matrimonial home fully insured at her > expense to its full replacement value against loss or damage by fire or other perils covered by a standard fire insurance extended coverage or additional perils supplemental contract and will apply any insurance proceeds to reasonable repairs. The insurance will cover both the husband's and the wife's interest in the matrimonial home. If the husband > demands it, the wife > will produce proof of premium payments and of the policy being in force. The husband and the wife will direct the insurer to send notices of premiums to both of them.>

>(>) The parties will bear equally the costs of major repairs to the matrimonial home, but only if the repairs are undertaken with the consent of both parties. No consent will be unreasonably withheld.>

(>) During the period of her > exclusive possession of the matrimonial home the wife > shall not change the use of the home, shall maintain its "principal residence" status within the meaning of the Income Tax Act, and shall so designate the home (and no other property) pursuant thereto. If the wife > contrary to this agreement sublets the matrimonial home, changes her > use of it, does not maintain its "principal residence" status for tax purposes, or does not designate it (and no other property) as her > principal residence with the result that the husband > becomes liable to pay any tax or penalty under the Income Tax Act, then the wife > agrees to indemnify the husband with respect to the liability or penalty.>

>(>) When the wife > is no longer entitled to exclusive possession of the matrimonial home, it will immediately be sold. Upon the sale of the matrimonial home the proceeds will be divided equally between the parties. Until the closing date of the sale of the matrimonial home, the wife > may continue to remain in exclusive possession of it. Any difference between the husband and wife on the method in terms of sale shall be resolved under the section of this

Agreement providing for the solution of differences.>

>(>) The husband and wife agree to divide the contents equally between them as they may agree.>

>(>) The husband and wife acknowledge that the contents have been divided between them to their mutual satisfaction and that each is entitled to the contents in his or her possession.>

>. HOUSEHOLD GOODS AND PERSONAL EFFECTS

Each of the parties acknowledges that:

(a) the contents of the matrimonial home, including furniture, furnishings, household goods, silverware, china, glassware, rugs, books, pictures, bric-a-brac and all other household effects have been divided between the parties or have been purchased or the value set off against the value of other property by one of the parties to the satisfaction of each of them;

(b) each has possession of his or her jewellery, clothing and personal effects;

(c) each may dispose of the items possessed by him or her as he or she deems fit.

>. DEBTS AND OBLIGATIONS

(1) Neither party will contract or incur debts or obligations in the name of the other.

(2) If, contrary to subsection (1), either party contracts or incurs debts or obligations in the name of the other, he or she will indemnify the other from all loss or expense that results from or is incidental to the transaction.

>. <u>RESUMPTION OF COHABITATION</u>

If at any time the parties cohabit as husband and wife for a single period or periods totally not more than ninety days with reconciliation as the primary purpose of the cohabitation, the provisions contained in this Agreement will not be affected except as provided in this section. If the parties cohabit as husband and wife for a single period or periods totalling not more than ninety days with reconciliation as the primary purpose of the cohabitation, the provisions contained in this Agreement will become void, except that nothing in the section will affect or invalidate any payment, conveyance or act made or done pursuant to the provisions of this Agreement.

_____   _____

>. <u>INDEPENDENT LEGAL ADVICE</u>

Each of the husband and the wife acknowledges that he or she:

(a) has had independent legal advice;

(b) understands his or her respective rights and obligations under this Agreement;

(c) is signing this Agreement voluntarily; and

(d) believes this Agreement is fair and reasonable and that its provisions are entirely adequate to discharge the present and future responsibilities of the parties and will not result in circumstances unconscionable to either party.

TO EVIDENCE THEIR AGREEMENT, each of the husband and the wife has signed this Agreement under seal before a witness.

SIGNED, SEALED AND DELIVERED)
   in the presence of:)
)
)

_____) _____

Witness as to the signature of) >
[wife's signature]
[wife] [Date]

_____) _____

Witness as to the signature of) >
[husband's signature]
[husband] [Date]

Caution: Parents, please do not attempt to adapt these contracts to your situation without the advice of a lawyer. Many of the clauses are alternatives to each other and would not necessarily be applicable to every case. These agreements also have an Ontario emphasis. They are reproduced as examples or guides only. Using them as drafting guides would be a good way to gather information about your situation.

Sample Certificates and Acknowledgements

CERTIFICATE AND ACKNOWLEDGEMENT

I have been consulted by husband [or wife] as to the legal effects of his [her] signing the within Marriage Contract.

I fully explained the nature of the agreement and the effect on his [her] rights of signing it. He [She] stated to me and I am satisfied that he [she] fully understands the nature and effect of the document and that he [she] executed it freely and voluntarily and not under any undue influence exercised by any other person. The importance of complete disclosure was explained.

Date: .... of ...., 19 ...

_____

(Solicitor)

   I hereby acknowledge that [solicitor] fully explained the nature of the agreement and the effect of my signing it. I confirm that I understand the nature and effect of the document, I have executed it freely and voluntarily. I have given complete disclosure and I am satisfied with the disclosure provided by my wife [husband].

Date: .... of ...., 19 ...

_____

(husband *or* wife)

(b) MARRIAGE CONTRACT

Marriage Contract Dated ....

B E T W E E N

Husband

....

And

....

Wife

MARRIAGE CONTRACT

RECITALS:

A. Whereas the parties intend to marry in the near future;

B. And Whereas they wish to opt out of the property and support regimes as established by the Common Law, Family Law Act, and the Divorce Act;

C. And Whereas their respective assets are listed in Schedule "A" and "B" attached, the values assigned to which are estimates only, neither party relying on specific accuracy of same for the purpose of this Agreement.

D. Now therefore they agree as follows:

1.1 Each party shall own his or her own property and may deal with it as he or she thinks fit, subject only to any restrictions imposed by Part II of the Family Law Act with respect to possession of a matrimonial home.

1.2 All property brought into the marriage shall be owned by spouse who owned it prior to the marriage and as established by Schedules "A" & "B".

1.3 For property acquired after marriage, ownership shall be conclusively established by the document that records ownership; but where no such document exists, by who has directly paid for the property, or where it is a gift, to whom the gift is given; and where none of the foregoing applies or can be ascertained, each shall be deemed one half owner as tenants-in-common of the property.

2. There shall be no property of a party included in his or her Net Family Property, so that each will always have Net Family Property equal to zero as contemplated by the Family Law Act or any successor legislation.

3. Neither party shall ever have any claim of any kind to property owned by the other, either alone or with a third person.

4. Contributions of any kind by way of money, labour, offering security or whatever from one spouse to help the other acquire, maintain, improve, dispose of or otherwise deal with property recorded in the other's name shall be conclusively deemed given without expectation of reimbursement or acquisition of an interest in the property of the other, and any kinds of claims that could be made based on such contributions are hereby waived and released.

5. Gifts from one to the other are absolute and the property received is the sole property of the receiving spouse.

6. Neither party shall have any claim to support from the other under any circumstances except as contemplated by paragraphs 6.2 and 6.3 (Insert circumstances if applicable).

7. If a separation should occur any property owned by both parties shall be divided between them equally (or otherwise if their interests are other than equal) in value, with value to be determined by an expert where the parties cannot agree, and if the parties cannot agree on the division of some or all property then the undivided properties shall be sold and the net proceeds divided in such a fashion as to ensure the division results in the parties sharing equally in total value the property unsold and the proceeds of sale.

8. Neither party shall have any claim of any kind against the estate of a dead spouse, except for claims based on bequests in wills, designation as beneficiaries in life insurance policies and death benefit plans, claims under this Agreement, and personal injury and property claims arising from negligence or willful conduct.

9. Each party shall be responsible for his or her own debts and will immediately reimburse each other for any payment and all costs and expenses associated therewith that he or she is called on to make and does not make for a debt which is the responsibility of the other. Where any liability is incurred by one

spouse in whole or in part with respect to property in which that spouse has no proprietary interest, the debt shall be deemed the debt of the property owner to the extent the debt was incurred relating to their property.

10. Each party has had independant legal advice and signs this Contract voluntarily.

11. Each party has made full disclosure of his or her significant assets, debts, liabilities and income.

12. The Contract will be interpreted in accordance with Ontario law, regardless of where the parties may reside.

13. Any word or terms of this Contract that are unenforceable or invalid will be deemed removed from the Agreement and the balance of the Agreement shall remain in force.

14. This Agreement shall apply whether the parties live together, separate, divorce or die.

15. The parties will execute any further documents necessary to give full effect to this Agreement.

16. No Agreement to vary this Contract is binding on the parties unless made in writing signed by the parties.

17. There are no representations, warranties, collateral agreements or conditions affecting this Agreement other than as set out in writing in this Agreement.

18. If the parties separate without entering into a written separation agreement and then reconcile and commence living together again then this Agreement shall continue to remain in effect as if parties had not separated.

19. This Contract shall only take effect upon the marriage of the parties.

20. This Agreement and any subsequent amendments shall ensue to the benefit of and be binding upon the parties' respective heirs, executors, administrators and assigns.

SIGNED THIS........of..........................., 199....

_____   _____
        Witness   (name of husband)

SIGNED THIS........of..........................., 199....

_____   _____
        Witness   (name of wife)

4. THE FINANCIAL STATEMENT

Much turns on this key statement about the individual's and the family's resources. It is an affidavit relating only to financial concerns. It summarizes financial abilities and liabilities. From these statements, which vary from province to province, the courts and the parties determine property division, spousal support, child support and even such issues as possession of the matrimonial home. The following form is from Ontario but the basic theory of dividing net worth is true for all provinces and the territories. For more information see Chapter 6, "Dividing The Family's Property."

Court File No.

ONTARIO COURT (GENERAL DIVISION)

BETWEEN:

Applicant

and

Respondent

FINANCIAL STATEMENT

I,   of the City of   MAKE OATH
AND SAY (or AFFIRM):

1.   Particulars of my financial situation and of all my property are accurately set out below, to the best of my knowledge, information and belief.

ALL INCOME & MONEY RECEIVED

(Include all income & other money received from all sources, whether taxable or not. Show gross amount here and show deductions on pages 3, 4, 5, & 6. Give current actual amount where known or ascertainable. Where amount cannot be ascertained, give your best estimate. Use weekly, monthly, & yearly column as appropriate.)

CATEGORY	WEEKLY	MONTHLY	YEARLY
1. Salary or Wages			
2. Bonuses			
3. Fees			
4. Commissions			
5. Child Tax Benefit			
6. Unemployment Insurance			
7. Workers' Compensation			
8. Public Assistance			
9. Pension			
10. Dividends			
11. Interest			
12. Rental Income			
13. Allowances & Support from others			
14. Other (Specify)			
TOTALS			

(Weekly Total) x (4.33)   = _____ monthly
(Monthly Total) x (1.00)   = _____ monthly
(Yearly Total) , (12.00)   = _____ monthly
GROSS MONTHLY INCOME = _____

OTHER BENEFITS

*(Show all non-monetary benefits from all sources, such as use of a
vehicle or room and board, and include such items as insurance or*

dental plans or other expenses paid on your behalf. Give your best estimate where you cannot ascertain the actual value.)

ITEM	PARTICULARS	MONTHLY MARKET VALUE
	TOTAL	

GROSS MONTHLY INCOME & BENEFITS _____

ACTUAL & PROPOSED BUDGETS

	ACTUAL BUDGET for twelve (12) month period FROM TO *Show actual expenses, or yourbest estimate where you ascertain the actual amount.*			PROPOSED BUDGET *Show your proposed budget, giving your best estimate where you cannot ascertain the actual amount.* Note: Increase Factor		
CATEGORY	Weekly	Monthly	Yearly	Weekly	Monthly	Yearly
HOUSING						
1. Rent						
2. Real property taxes						
3. Mortgage						
4. Common expenses						
5. Water						
6. Electricity						
7. Natural gas						

	ACTUAL BUDGET			PROPOSED BUDGET		
CATEGORY	Weekly	Monthly	Yearly	Weekly	Monthly	Yearly
8. Fuel oil						
9. Telephone						
10. Cable T.V.						
11. Home Insurance						
12. Repairs and maintenance						
13. Gardening and snow removal						
14. Other— specify						
FOOD, TOILETRIES & SUNDRIES						
15. Groceries						
16. Meals outside home						
17. Toiletries & sundries						
18. Grooming						
19. General household supplies						
20. Laundry, dry cleaning						

	ACTUAL BUDGET			PROPOSED BUDGET		
CATEGORY	Weekly	Monthly	Yearly	Weekly	Monthly	Yearly
21. Other—specify						
CLOTHING						
22. Children						
23. Self						
TRANSPORTATION						
24. Public transit						
25. Taxis, car pool						
26. Car insurance						
27. Licence						
28. Car maintenance						
29. Gasoline, oil						
30. Parking						
31. Other—specify						
HEALTH & MEDICAL						
32. Doctors, chiropractors						
33. Dentist (regular care)						

	ACTUAL BUDGET			PROPOSED BUDGET		
CATEGORY	Weekly	Monthly	Yearly	Weekly	Monthly	Yearly
34. Orthodontist, or special dental care						
35. Insurance premiums						
36. Drugs						
37. Other— specify						
DEDUCTIONS FROM INCOME						
38. Income tax						
39. Canada Pension						
40. Unemployment insurance						
41. Employer pension						
42. Union or other dues						
43. Group insurance						
44. Credit union loan						

	ACTUAL BUDGET			PROPOSED BUDGET		
CATEGORY	Weekly	Monthly	Yearly	Weekly	Monthly	Yearly
45. Credit union savings						
46. Other— specify						
MISCELLANEOUS						
47. Life insurance premiums						
48. Tuition fees, books, etc.						
49. Entertainment						
50. Recreation						
51. Vacation						
52. Gifts						
53. Babysitting, day care						
54. Children's allowances						
55. Children's activities						
56. Support payments						
57. Newspapers, periodicals						

CATEGORY	ACTUAL BUDGET			PROPOSED BUDGET		
	Weekly	Monthly	Yearly	Weekly	Monthly	Yearly
58. Alcohol, tobacco						
59. Charities						
60. Income tax (not deducted at source)						
61. Other— specify						
LOAN PAYMENTS						
62. Banks						
63. Finance companies						
64. Credit unions						
65. Department stores						
66. Other— specify						
SAVINGS						
67. RRSP/RSP						
68. Other— specify						
TOTALS						

TOTALS OF ACTUAL BUDGET TOTALS OF PROPOSED BUDGET

Monthly Total x 1	=	Monthly Total x 1 =
Weekly Total x 4.33	=	Weekly Total x 4.33 =
Yearly Total , 12	=	Yearly Total , 12 =

_____   _____

MONTHLY ACTUAL BUDGET MONTHLY PROPOSED BUDGET

_____   _____

SUMMARY OF INCOME &   SUMMARY OF INCOME &
EXPENSES ACTUAL   EXPENSES PROPOSED

Gross monthly income		Gross monthly income
Subtract Actual -		Subtract Proposed -
monthly budget		monthly budget

_____   _____

ACTUAL MONTHLY   PROPOSED MONTHLY
SURPLUS / (DEFICIT)_____ SURPLUS / (DEFICIT)_____

LAND

(Include any interest in land owned on the valuation date, including leasehold interests and mortgages, whether or not you are registered as owner. Include claims to an interest in land, but do not include claims that you are making against your spouse in this or a related proceeding. Show estimated market value of your interest without deducting encumbrances or costs of disposition, and show encumbrances and costs of disposition under Debts and Other Liabilities on page 280.)

NATURE & TYPE OF OWNERSHIP	NATURE & ADDRESS OF PROPERTY	ESTIMATED MARKET VALUE OF YOUR INTEREST AS OF: *(See instructions above)*	
(State percentage interest where relevant.)	DATE OF MARRIAGE **Date:** Matrimonial Home	VALUATION DATE	DATE OF STATEMENT
TOTALS			

GENERAL HOUSEHOLD ITEMS & VEHICLES

(Show estimated market value, not cost of replacement for these items owned on the valuation date. Do not deduct encumbrances here but show encumbrances under Debts and Other Liabilities on page 280.)

ITEM	PARTICULARS	ESTIMATED MARKET VALUE OF YOUR INTEREST AS OF: (See instructions above)		
		DATE OF MARRIAGE	VALUATION DATE	DATE OF STATEMENT
General household contents including special items				
a) matrimonial home(s)				
b) elsewhere				
Jewellery				
Works of art				
Vehicles & boats				
Other special items				
TOTALS				

SAVINGS & SAVINGS PLANS

(Show items owned on the valuation date by category. Include cash, accounts in financial institutions, registered retirement or other savings plans, deposit receipts, pensions and any other savings.)

| CATEGORY | INSTITUTION | ACCOUNT NUMBER | AMOUNT AS OF: | | |
			DATE OF MARRIAGE	VALUATION DATE	DATE OF STATEMENT
	TOTALS				

SECURITIES

(Show items owned on the valuation date by category. Include shares, bonds, warrants, options, debentures, notes and any other securities. Give your best estimate of market value if the items were to be sold on the open market.)

| CATEGORY | INSTITUTION | ACCOUNT NUMBER | AMOUNT AS OF: | | |
			DATE OF MARRIAGE	VALUATION DATE	DATE OF STATEMENT
	TOTALS				

LIFE & DISABILITY INSURANCE

(List all policies owned on the valuation date.)

| Company & Policy | Kind of Policy | Owner Beneficiary | $ Face Value | CASH SURRENDER VALUE AS OF: | | |
				Date of Marriage	Valuation Date	Date Of Statement
			TOTALS			

ACCOUNTS RECEIVABLE

(Give particulars of all debts owing to you on the valuation date, whether arising from business or from personal dealings.)

PARTICULARS		AMOUNT AS OF:		
		DATE OF MARRIAGE	VALUATION DATE	DATE OF STATEMENT
	TOTALS			

BUSINESS INTERESTS

(Show any interest in an unincorporated business owned on the valuation date. A controlling interest in an incorporated business may be shown here or under Securities on page 9. Give your best estimate of market value if the business were to be sold on an open market.)

NAME OF FIRM OR COMPANY	INTEREST	ESTIMATED MARKET VALUE AS OF:		
		DATE OF MARRIAGE	VALUATION DATE	DATE OF STATEMENT
	TOTALS			

OTHER PROPERTY

(Show other property owned on valuation date by categories. Include property of any kind not shown above. Give your best estimate of market value.)

CATEGORY	PARTICULARS	ESTIMATED MARKET VALUE AS OF:		
		DATE OF MARRIAGE	VALUATION DATE	DATE OF STATEMENT
	TOTALS			

DEBTS & OTHER LIABILITIES

(Show your debts and liabilities on the valuation date, whether arising from personal or business dealings, by category such as mortgages, charges, liens, credit cards, notes and accounts payable. Include contingent liabilities such as guarantees and indicate that they are contingent.)

CATEGORY	PARTICULARS	ESTIMATED MARKET VALUE AS OF:		
		DATE OF MARRIAGE	VALUATION DATE	DATE OF STATEMENT
	TOTALS			

PROPERTY, DEBTS & OTHER LIABILITIES ON DATE OF MARRIAGE

(Show by category the value of your property and your debts and other liabilities calculated as of the date of your marriage. Do not include the value of a matrimonial home that you owned at the date of marriage.)

CATEGORY	PARTICULARS	VALUE AS OF MARRIAGE DATE:	
		ASSETS	LIABILITIES
Land, excludes matrimonial home owned on date of marriage			
General household items and vehicles			
Savings and savings plans			
Securities			
Life and disability insurance			
Accounts receivable			
Business interests			
Other property			
Debts and other liabilities			
	TOTALS		
NET VALUE OF PROPERTY OWNED ON DATE OF MARRIAGE =			

EXCLUDED PROPERTY

(Show the value by category of property owned on the valuation date that is excluded from the definition of "net family property.")

CATEGORY	PARTICULARS	VALUE ON VALUATION DATE
	TOTALS	

DISPOSAL OF PROPERTY

(Show the value by category of all property that you disposed of during the two years immediately preceding the making of this statement, or during the marriage, whichever period is shorter.)

CATEGORY	PARTICULARS	VALUE
	TOTALS	

CALCULATION OF NET FAMILY PROPERTY

Value of all property owned on valuation date

Subtract value of all deductions   −

Subtract value of all excluded property   −

　　　　　　　　　NET FAMILY PROPERTY $

2. The name(s) and address(es) of my employer(s) are:

3. Attached to this affidavit are a copy of my income tax return filed with the Department of National Revenue for the last taxation year, together with all material filed with it, and a copy of any notice of assessment or reassessment that I have received from the Department for that year.

4. I do not anticipate any material changes in the information set out above.

4. I anticipate the following changes in the information set out above.

Sworn before me at the   )
)
<— City name here   )
)
<— Municipality name here   )
)
<— Date here   )
)
) _____
                                          Signature

_____
Commissioner for Taking Affidavits etc.

Glossary of Common Legal Terms

There are many unusual words that may be used during a separation and divorce. In this section of the Appendices, I have selected a few of the more common terms and tried to provide some definitions that you can understand.

Access The time set aside for a parent who does not have custody and his or her children to spend time with each other. It can also include the right of a parent to information about the children's health, education and welfare. The time can be very specific (e.g., "every weekend from Saturday at 9 a.m. to Sunday at 7 p.m.") or very vague (e.g., "liberal and generous access as may be agreed from time to time").

Adultery Sexual intercourse by a husband or wife with someone of the opposite sex who is not his or her spouse. It is one of the reasons that a court will give a divorce.

Adversarial System Canada's court system is designed to deal with disputes between two parties who oppose each other. Each side tries to prove what they say happened and what they want the judge to order. The judge is neutral and listens to both sides. He or she will decide which is correct, apply the law and make an order or give a judgment.

Affidavit A statement that is written down and a person swears is true. It must be witnessed. The court sometimes reads these statements to get evidence.

Alimony An old expression that really means the same thing as spousal support.

Annulment When a judge declares that a marriage was never valid to begin with. It may be invalid because it was not consummated or because one of the people was tricked into the marriage, or was insane or didn't understand what they were doing. A religious annulment permits divorced people to marry again within the faith.

Appeal If a person who is affected by a judge's decision thinks that the judge made a mistake, then that person may ask a higher court to take another look at the decision. The higher court might order a new trial, fix the decision or leave it alone.

Battered To be beaten, harassed, or threatened. See **Domestic Violence**.

Best Interests Test This is the test that the judge will apply in deciding anything that affects children. It involves asking, "What is best for this child?"

Child The *Divorce Act* says that a "child of the marriage" is any child towards whom the spouses act as a parent. (Spouses include biological parents and stepparents and even common-law spouses who treated a child as if he or she was their own.) If someone treats a person as if they were a child then he or she may be considered a parent of the child. Usually, "child" means being under 16 or under the age of majority for the province in which the child lives. In the case of support, though, a "child" can include a young person right to the time that person gets his or her first university degree. It can also include older kids who are too ill or unable to care for themselves.

Cohabitation Agreement A contract signed by a man and a woman who are living together or plan to live together. In the contract they may agree to what the rules will be while they live together or what will happen if they split up. They are not permitted to agree about what will happen to the children if the man and woman separate because it is too difficult to predict what children will need in the future.

Common-Law Spouse Almost all the provinces and territories recognize that a man and a woman may want to live together without getting married. Some provinces give these couples the right to claim spousal support if the relationship ends. The length of time that they must live together in order to be called common-law spouses varies from province to province.

Confidentiality A person who retains a lawyer has the right to have that lawyer keep everything a secret. Even a judge cannot order the lawyer to violate lawyer-client confidentiality.

Consummation of Marriage The final step to having a valid marriage — an act of sexual intercourse. If this does not occur then a couple's marriage can be annulled.

Contempt To disobey a judge's order on purpose. Punishable by a fine or jail term.

Contested Divorce If either the husband or the wife disputes the grounds for the divorce or if parents cannot agree on terms, then a judge may have to decide for them. A hearing or trial may need to be held.

Costs The expense of all the legal proceedings. If one person loses the case, then the judge may order that person to pay some or all of the lawyers' fees and expenses of the other side.

Discoveries A step in a case going through the court system. At this step the lawyers get to ask the clients about the case. It happens well in advance of the court trial and allows each side to "discover" what evidence the other side has.

Divorce A judge's decision that a legal marriage is ended or dissolved.

Domestic Violence The intent by one spouse to intimidate, either by threat or by use of physical force on the other spouse.

Fees and Disbursements The lawyer's bill — made up of what the lawyer charges for her or his time and the out-of-pocket expenses, like photocopies.

Garnishee A legal procedure that allows the court to seize a person's money or property if that person owes money and has not repaid it.

Indexing Increasing the amount of support each year to keep up with the cost of living.
Interim Orders It takes a long time to get something through the courts to a final decision. Until the final order is made, the judge may make an order in the meantime — in the interim.

Joint Custody When a mother and father agree to share the physical and/or legal responsibility for their children after the separation and divorce.

Joint Petition If a man and a woman agree that they should get a divorce, it is possible for them to complete one document together asking for a divorce. This is called a Joint Petition for Divorce. See Appendix II.

Judgment The judge's final decision in a case.

Litigation Using the court process to dispute a matter; eventually asking a judge to decide the issue.

Marriage A voluntary joining of one man and one woman into a legal bond for life, to the exclusion of all others. A valid marriage must meet all the rules of the place where the ceremony was held.

Marriage Breakdown The sole ground for a divorce being ordered by the judge. A marriage breakdown can be proven by showing that the husband and wife have lived apart for one year, that one of them committed adultery or that there was physical or mental cruelty.

Marriage Contract A contract between a man and a woman who are married or who will be married. Usually the couple sets out the rules for their marriage or what will happen if they separate and divorce.

Matrimonial Home The home in which a legally married husband and wife lived during their marriage.

Mediation A process used by people who have a conflict in which a neutral third person assists them in finding a solution that meets everyone's needs.

Minutes of Settlement A document in which people who have been in litigation write out the points of the agreement to settle their dispute.

Motion A request that the judge decide something for the people in litigation. For instance, one parent may put forward a motion to increase child support.

Order The judge's decision to resolve a dispute between sides in a divorce. Many orders may be made during the litigation, but only one final judgment is made at the end.

Parties The people involved in the litigation or the dispute. Anyone who is asking the judge to make an order.

Petition for Divorce The document that a husband or wife uses to ask the judge to give him or her a divorce.

Pleadings The documents exchanged by the parties in the litigation. Each side summarizes what they think happened and what they want the judge to order.

Restraining Order An order that requires one spouse to stay away from the other spouse and possibly the children. This can happen if the court thinks there may be violence or trouble if the two people are near each other. If it is disobeyed, the judge will punish the offender with a fine or jail term.

Retainer The contract that a client uses to hire a lawyer, usually including some money.

Separate To split up. It may involve one spouse moving out, but it is possible for a husband and wife to live separate in the same house. To do so, they stop sleeping together, eating meals together and basically lead separate lives. This starts the clock for a divorce based on a one-year separation.

Separation Agreement A contract between a husband and wife (or a common-law couple) in which they agree to settle all of the things they need to clear up after a separation and usually before a divorce. These include issues such as custody, access, support and property division.

Shared Parenting See **Joint Custody**.

Solicitor-Client Privilege The rule that says a lawyer must keep everything that the client tells him or her confidential. A lawyer may break the rule only to prevent a crime from occurring or to report child abuse.

Spousal Support Money paid after separation by one spouse to the other to help the spouse meet expenses until he or she no longer needs help. It can be for a while (until the spouse has found a job or has been retrained) or it can go on indefinitely.
Spouse A legal term for a husband or wife, including common-law couples.

Statute A law that has been passed by the province or federal Parliament, like the *Divorce Act.*

Uncontested Divorce If the husband and wife agree that they both want a divorce, and if they can agree on all the matters affecting the children and the property, then the divorce is not opposed by either of them. It is uncontested.

Variation The procedure used to go back to a judge and ask him or her to change an order that was made earlier. It is not an appeal. In a variation the change is sought because circumstances have changed (e.g., a support payment needs to be lowered because the person paying it lost his or her job).

INDEX